TIMEFORM HORSES TO FOLLOW

2025/26 JUMPS SEASON

with SPORTING LIFE

CONTENTS

TIMEFORM'S FIFTY TO FOLLOW 2025/26	**3**
HORSES TO FOLLOW FROM IRELAND	**55**
LOOKING AHEAD	**75**
Patrick Mullins' Horses To Follow	76
Daryl Jacob's Horses To Follow	78
Talking To The Trainers	80
Rising Stars	87
Stable Switchers	92
Ante-Post Betting	97
REVIEW OF 2024/25	**103**
Timeform's View	104
2024/25 Statistics (Britain)	130
REFERENCE & INDEX	**131**
The Timeform Top 100	132
Index	134

TIMEFORM

© TIMEFORM LIMITED 2025
COPYRIGHT AND LIABILITY

Copyright in all Timeform Publications is strictly reserved by the Publishers and no material therein may be reproduced stored in a retrieval system or transmitted in any form or by any means electronic mechanical photocopying recording or otherwise without written permission of Timeform Limited.

Timeform Horses To Follow is published by Timeform Limited, 4 Wellington Place, Leeds, LS1 4AP (e-mail: help@timeform.com). It is supplied to the purchaser for his personal use and on the understanding that its contents are not disclosed. Except where the purchaser is dealing as a consumer (as defined in the Unfair Contract Terms Act 1977 Section 12) all conditions warranties or terms relating to fitness for purpose merchantability or condition of the goods and whether implied by Statute Common Law or otherwise are excluded and no responsibility is accepted by the Publishers for any loss whatsoever caused by any acts errors or omissions whether negligent or otherwise of the Publishers their Servants Agents or otherwise.

ISBN 978-1-9192502-0-5 Price £14.95

Printed and bound by
Weatherbys Ltd
Sanders Road
Wellingborough
NN8 4BX

SECTION 1

Timeform's Fifty To Follow, carefully chosen by Timeform and Sporting Life editorial staff, are listed below with their respective page numbers. A selection of ten (**marked in bold with a ★**) is made for those who prefer a smaller list.

ACE OF SPADES (FR)	4	LE TIEP'S SACRE (FR) ★	29
BATTLE BORN LAD	5	**LULAMBA (FR)** ★	29
BE AWARE (FR)	6	MIAMI MAGIC (IRE)	31
BORN IN THE WEST (IRE)	7	**MYDADDYPADDY (IRE)** ★	32
BURNING IT UP (IRE)	8	MYRETOWN (IRE)	33
CALIFET EN VOL (IRE)	8	NO DRAMA THIS END (IRE)	34
CELTIC DINO (FR)	10	OUR BOY STAN	35
CHASINGOUTTHEBLUES (IRE) ★	11	**REALCO** ★	37
CONMAN JOHN (IRE)	12	RUBBER BALL	38
DEDICATED HERO (IRE)	13	SKUNA BAY (IRE)	39
DERRYHASSEN PADDY (IRE) ★	14	SOLDIER'S LEAP (IRE)	40
DIVA LUNA (IRE)	15	SOME BRO (IRE)	41
GEORGE'S LAD (IRE)	16	STARZAND (IRE)	41
HAITI COULEURS (FR)	17	STRONG RUN	42
IDAHO SUN (IRE)	18	TERRORISE	43
JAGWAR (FR) ★	19	THE NEW LION	44
JANGO BAIE (FR)	20	TOM DONIPHON (FR)	45
JESUILA DES MOTTES (FR)	22	TUTTI QUANTI (FR)	46
JOB (FR)	22	VANDERPOEL (IRE)	47
JUBY BALL (FR) ★	23	WALK TALL (IRE)	49
JUPITER DES BORDES (FR)	24	WELLINGTON ARCH	50
KABRAL DU MATHAN (FR)	25	WENDIGO (FR)	50
KEPLER'S LAW	26	WILSTAR (IRE)	51
KINGSTON QUEEN (IRE)	27	**WOLF MOON** ★	52
LAST RODEO (IRE)	28	**YOUNG GETAWAY (IRE)** ★	54

The form summary for each horse is shown after its age, colour, sex and pedigree. The summary shows the distance, the state of the going and where the horse finished in each of its races since the start of the 2024/25 season. Performances are in chronological sequence with the date of its last race shown at the end (F-ran on Flat).

The distance of each race is given in furlongs. Steeplechase form figures are prefixed by the letter 'c', hurdle form figures by the letter 'h' and NH Flat race or bumper form figures by the letter 'b'.

The going is symbolised as follows: f–firm, m–good to firm; g–good, d–good to soft; s–soft; v–heavy.

Placings are indicated, up to the sixth place, by use of superior figures, an asterisk being used to denote a win and superior letters are used to convey what happened to a horse during the race: F–fell, pu–pulled up, ur–unseated rider, bd–brought down, su–slipped up, ro–ran out.

The Timeform Rating of a horse is simply the merit of the horse expressed in pounds and is arrived at by careful examination of its running against other horses. The ratings range from 175+ for the champions down to a figure of around 55 for selling platers. Symbols attached to the ratings: 'p'–likely to improve; 'P'–capable of much better form; '+'–the horse may be better than we have rated it.

Ace of Spades (Fr) h126

6 b.g. Dink (Fr) – Alinga's Lass (Ire) (Whipper (USA))
2024/25 h15.8d⁴ h18.5d² h16.4d* h22.7d* h20.9d⁴ h24.3g² Apr 11

Dan Skelton has enjoyed success at the top level with jumpers from a variety of backgrounds but one who had more 'left field' origins than most was Nube Negra, a maiden on the Flat in Spain before joining Skelton. But Nube Negra soon proved useful over hurdles and was then better still as a two-mile chaser, winning the Desert Orchid Chase, two editions of the Shloer Chase and finishing a half-length second to Put The Kettle On in the 2021 Queen Mother Champion Chase. Nube Negra proved such a good advert for his little-known sire Dink, then standing in France, that he was bought to become the first stallion for Dan and Grace Skelton's Alne Park Stud. Dink's first British-bred foals are yet to hit the track, but he's now had a handful of winners in Britain, including Ace of Spades who, as Nube Negra did, looks the type to go on to better things for the Skelton yard over fences.

Ace of Spades progressed to win the last of his three starts in bumpers, at Warwick, before switching to hurdles last season. The four-runner maiden he won at Cheltenham's November meeting was an ordinary race for the track and he had to work hard to justify favouritism, but that was over two miles and he looked more comfortable, despite the strong headwind, when following up in a novice at Kelso the following month over an extra three quarters of a mile. In landing the odds by six and a half lengths from Far From Over, Ace of Spades initiated a treble for his stable's three runners on the card.

Moving into handicaps in the spring, Ace of Spades showed improved form in defeat. Back at Kelso, he shaped encouragingly over a slightly shorter trip when staying on late for fourth behind Bold Light and matched that effort stepped up to three miles at Ayr where he very nearly ended the season on a winning note, challenging from two out and edged out only in the final 50 yards by Billy Boi Blue who beat him a head. A strong gelding and the type to make a chaser, Ace of Spades is a half-brother to the Tolworth Novices' Hurdle winner Tahmuras who himself made into a useful chaser in the same Noel Fehily Racing Syndicates colours. **Dan Skelton**

Conclusion: *Chasing type who progressed over hurdles, proving suited by longer distances, and remains unexposed over three miles*

Battle Born Lad   h128

6 b.g. Califet (Fr) – Cute N You Know It (Tamure (Ire))
2024/25 b16.2g³ h16.2s* h24.3d* h24.7g^{pu} Apr 4

Battle Born Lad still looked a work in progress over hurdles last season but that didn't stop him winning a Grade 2 novice and it should have laid the foundations for a successful chasing career. He certainly has the size for fences, being a tall, chasing type, and the fact that he was still raw and inexperienced last term should mean there's still plenty of improvement to come from him over the larger obstacles. Battle Born Lad was placed in all three of his bumpers, the first two at Newcastle in the spring of the 2023/24 season and the third one being the valuable final in the Go North Series at Kelso which was rescued from an abandoned card earlier in the year and run early last season in May. Making the running as usual, Battle Born Lad was headed over two furlongs out but was rallying at the finish to be third behind Dedicated Hero, another who would go on to Grade 2 success as a novice hurdler later in the season and earn a place in this year's book.

Battle Born Lad made a successful debut over hurdles in a novice at Hexham in October over two miles where he and the runner-up pulled a long way clear of the rest. That form looked all the better after the second, Wendigo, filled the same place behind The New Lion in the Grade 1 Challow at Newbury in late-December (both are among our *Fifty*, incidentally). Battle Born Lad wasn't seen out again, though, until February when he was upped markedly in trip for the Prestige Novices' Hurdle at Haydock. That race lost some of its interest due to late withdrawals, but Battle Born Lad showed improved form over the longer trip, even if he did enjoy the run of things.

Battle Born Lad's inexperience was evident both during and after the race as he ran wide on the bends, as he had done in one of his bumpers, and unseated his rider after the line. But barring an untidy jump at the last where he was already in control in any case, he jumped well and pulled away again to win by five and a half lengths from the favourite Moon Rocket. The first two met again in the Sefton Novices' Hurdle at Aintree but neither gave their running and were pulled up. Even so, with more maturity Battle Born Lad has the makings of a smart chaser. **Mark Walford**

Conclusion: *Still something of a raw talent over hurdles but showed plenty of ability and shouldn't have any trouble winning races over fences in the North*

Be Aware (Fr) h133

6 gr.g. Martaline – Kendova (Fr) (Kendor (Fr))
2024/25 h16.4d² h15.7d³ h21d h20g Apr 4

If this is an unsuccessful selection we can't say we weren't warned. He failed to win when picked for last season's edition of *Horses To Follow*, he left plenty of burnt fingers when only eighth in the Coral Cup having been sent off the shortest-priced favourite for the race this century, and he's even called Be Aware! However, we are retaining the faith in a handicapper that still has untapped potential, especially at trips around two miles.

The season almost started perfectly for Be Aware who was beaten only half a length by Burdett Road in the valuable Greatwood Handicap Hurdle at Cheltenham's November meeting. That was a cracking effort in receipt of only 3 lb from a race-fit rival who would go on to show smart form in graded company, though Be Aware was unable to build on that promise and was a beaten favourite on his three subsequent outings, starting with the Ladbrokes Hurdle at Ascot where he was only third.

He was especially strong in the market for the Coral Cup at the Cheltenham Festival where, upped in trip, he was sent off at only 3/1 in a 26-runner field. His backers would have been on good terms with themselves coming down the hill as Be Aware easily made headway to get into a challenging position, and he was right in the firing line on the turn into the straight. However, he failed to pick up when asked and ultimately finished only eighth. It was a similar story in another valuable handicap hurdle at Aintree where he filled the same position, though he never got quite so competitive after pulling hard in the early stages, and he was ultimately beaten a fair bit further.

Be Aware had finished runner-up in a 21-furlong novice hurdle the previous season but seemed to find his stamina stretched by similar trips in ultra-competitive handicaps at major spring festivals. The way he went through those races at Cheltenham and Aintree suggest he'll appreciate a return to around two miles, while his Timeform description of raw-boned gelding offers hope that he might return from a break as a more mature and stronger model. He's a chaser on looks and it could be that fences will be the making of him. **Dan Skelton**

Conclusion: *Failed to meet expectations after making a promising start over hurdles but is in excellent hands to fulfil his potential and appeals as useful chasing prospect; should benefit from a drop in trip*

Born In The West (Ire) h102

6 gr.g. Westerner – Lucinda Grey (Ire) (Luso)
2024/25 b16.8g² b16g⁶ h15.8g⁵ h15.8s h16s³ h19.9s² h20.4s² h19.3m* h27d² h24.3g³ Apr 19

With ten runs last season, Born In The West was one of the busier members of this *Fifty* but there are good grounds for thinking he has more to offer in his second season under Rules. For one thing, he generally progressed with racing, improvement which went hand in hand with having his stamina tested more, and he remains unexposed as a stayer after only a couple of runs at three miles or further. There's also the prospect of further improvement to come when Born In The West tackles fences as he's a winning pointer and a workmanlike, chasing type in appearance.

Born In The West began the season with a couple of runs in bumpers in the summer for David Pipe and went close to making a winning debut at Newton Abbot. After a five-month break, he returned for a new yard, Sam England's West Yorkshire stable, and made a low-key start to his hurdling career over two miles. But when stepped up to around two and a half miles after the turn of the year, Born In The West began to show a bit more ability and finished second in a couple of ordinary handicaps at Sedgefield and Southwell. Progressing again, he went one better in a similar event at Catterick in March where he produced a particularly good round of jumping before asserting on the run-in to justify favouritism and beat Rehill Relic by a length and a quarter.

Although beaten at short odds in his two remaining starts, Born In The West ran his best races all season stepping up to three miles or more. The first of those was at Sedgefield over three miles and three furlongs. Seeing it out well, Born In The West went down to another improving type in Musique de Fee whilst pulling a long way clear of the rest. There was less emphasis on stamina in a steadily-run novice handicap at Haydock on his final start, but he turned in another good effort to be beaten around a length into third after conceding first run. **Sam England**

Conclusion: *Improved with racing, particularly when stepped up in trip, and looks the type to do better still over fences*

Burning It Up (Ire)   h95+

5 b.g. Milan – Burnt It Up (Ire) (Scorpion (Ire))
2024/25 b16.2d⁵ h16.2d⁵ h16s⁴ h16.2s³ h20.2s² Apr 25

Burning It Up showed some promise in his first season under Rules north of the border, but he's only five and isn't bred to come into his own until he tackles longer distances and probably fences, too. Burning It Up, purchased for £35,000 after finishing third on his sole start in Irish points, looked in need of the experience when making his bumper debut at Kelso in the autumn. He was then kept to two miles for his first three runs over hurdles and shaped as though further would suit.

His best run duly came when he was stepped up to two and a half miles for his handicap debut in a novice event at the Perth Festival in April. He bumped into a winner on a sharp upward curve but Burning It Up ran creditably, faring best of the rest albeit 14 lengths behind Scorsese. With the winner jumping boldly in front and making all the running, Burning It Up chased him throughout but was one paced in the closing stages having made a mistake three out.

By Milan out of an unraced daughter of another St Leger winner, Scorpion, Burning It Up will stay further still in due course. His grandam Burn Out was a fairly useful hurdler and as well as being the dam of winning staying chaser Miss Serious, she's also the grandam of Gaillimh A Stor who is a fairly useful staying hurdler for Burning It Up's connections but hasn't taken to fences quite so well, despite starting favourite to beat Myretown on the same Kelso card where Burning It Up finished third on his penultimate start. Hopefully, Burning It Up will fare better over fences himself, though it's still early days for him and there could be staying handicaps over hurdles to be won with him first. **Nick Alexander**

Conclusion: *Showed promise over hurdles, notably when stepped up in trip for his handicap debut on his final start, and there's likely more to come when faced with sterner tests of stamina*

Califet En Vol (Ire)   h132

6 br.g. Califet (Fr) – Mallards In Flight (Ire) (Well Chosen)
2024/25 h21d* h20.5d² h19.6d* h24.7g⁶ Apr 4

Califet En Vol was only sixth of eight finishers in the Sefton Novices' Hurdle at Aintree, but it says plenty about the promising start he'd made to his career that he was sent off the 3/1 favourite on his first crack at a Grade 1. Califet En Vol pulled too hard to be a factor in the finish on his first start over three miles, but he remains likely to stay that trip given a bit more time to mature, and it is as a staying novice chaser that he is expected to thrive this season.

Califet En Vol did too much too soon in the Sefton but remains a fine prospect for chasing

Califet En Vol, who was purchased for £145,000 after finishing runner-up on his only appearance in Irish points, started out under Rules at the 2024 Scottish Grand National meeting in a bumper that Nicky Henderson historically targeted with some talented prospects, most notably Sprinter Sacre who went on to become Timeform's highest-rated chaser of the modern era. Henderson had won that Ayr bumper a remarkable five times between 2010 and 2017, but, prior to Califet En Vol, had been represented only twice since 2018. Califet En Vol was unable to add his name to the honour roll, but he offered plenty to work with in third, despite understandably displaying signs of inexperience. Califet En Vol showed enough at Ayr to suggest he'd have little problem winning a bumper, but he was sent straight over hurdles after returning from a summer break, and he created a superb impression at Kempton in November. Looking much sharper than he had on debut, Califet En Vol tanked his way into the lead between the final two flights and readily extended the advantage up the run-in to score by 15 lengths with his rider hardly having to move.

He had to settle for second on his next outing at Newbury a few weeks later, but that three-length defeat—which hardly constituted a disappointing effort at the time—looked much better by the end of the season given the winner, The New Lion, went on to claim Grade 1s on his two subsequent starts and ended the campaign as Timeform's highest-rated novice hurdler. Califet En Vol faced nothing of The New Lion's calibre when next seen in the listed Sidney Banks Memorial Novices' Hurdle, though he was still up against some useful types and had to work hard to get the verdict by half a length. There was a lot to like about how Califet En Vol responded to pressure to grind his way to the front up the run-in, having jumped the last a length down in third, and that performance offers plenty of hope he will stay further than two and a half miles, for all he didn't prove that theory in better company at Aintree. **Nicky Henderson**

Conclusion: *Created a good impression before pulling too hard on his first crack at three miles at Aintree; looks worth another go at that trip and should make up into a useful novice chaser*

Celtic Dino (Fr) h134

6 ch.g. Doctor Dino (Fr) – Bal Celtique (Fr) (Ballingarry (Ire))
2024/25 h15.2g* h15.7g* h17s⁴ h16s³ h16.5g³ Apr 4

Not many jockeys land a retainer with a leading owner whilst still being able to claim, but conditional Dylan Johnston was given that opportunity when appointed number-one jockey to Dai Walters in the summer of 2024. Winning the Swinton Handicap Hurdle at Haydock on the Olly Murphy-trained Pickanumber a few months earlier must have been a good advertisement for Johnston's talent. However, Johnston had already had a high-profile ride for Sam Thomas, who trains most of Walters' horses, when partnering former race winner Iwilldoit to finish third in the 2023 Welsh Grand National. It wasn't long before Johnston landed a good prize in his new role, winning the Welsh Champion Hurdle at Ffos Las aboard the smart Lump Sum on whom he also finished runner-up in the Fighting Fifth Hurdle and William Hill Hurdle later in the season.

The Thomas stable's runners often hit the ground running in the autumn and another who made a strong start to the season was Celtic Dino. The winner of two of his three bumpers, Celtic Dino won his first two races over hurdles under Johnston, a maiden at Wincanton and then an intermediate contest at Ascot the following month in which he led from the second flight and kept on well on the run-in. While Celtic Dino didn't add to those successes, he made the frame in his remaining starts, including in graded company on his next two outings. He wasn't at all discredited when fourth to Potters Charm in the Formby Novices' Hurdle at Aintree and then ran better when third behind Tripoli Flyer in the Dovecote Novices' Hurdle at Kempton. But his best effort came when well backed for his handicap debut in the conditional jockeys' and amateur riders' hurdle at the Grand National meeting. After suffering early interference, Celtic Dino recovered and briefly looked set to take command in the straight, but he was headed in the final furlong and finished third behind She's A Saint.

The tall, well-made Celtic Dino is a chaser on looks and bred to do better over fences as he's a half-brother to Saint Segal who had a good season in handicap chases up to two and a half miles last term. Raced only around two miles to date, and mostly on easy tracks at that, he can improve for stiffer tests. **Sam Thomas**

Conclusion: *Chasing type who reached a useful level over hurdles, including when third in a competitive handicap at Aintree, and can do better over fences, especially when stepped up in trip*

Chasingouttheblues (Ire)   h116
6 b.g. Sea Moon – Bally Tutu (Ire) (Shantou (USA))
2024/25 h17.1s⁵ h20.1d* h19.3s h19.7s* h24.3s* h24.3d³ h23.3s h24.3g⁶ Apr 11

Jockey Jamie Hamilton enjoyed another good season in 2024/25, with a total of 32 winners which matched his previous best score set in the preceding campaign. He also had his first graded winner, with Battle Born Lad, another of this season's *Fifty*, winning the Prestige Novices' Hurdle at Haydock. Hamilton also enjoyed plenty of success on another of Mark Walford's novice hurdlers, Chasingouttheblues, riding him in all his races and winning three times.

Chasingouttheblues shaped as though in need of further on his debut over hurdles at Carlisle and duly got off the mark at the second attempt when stepped up to two and a half miles for a maiden at Hexham. While he underperformed back at Carlisle next time, he soon resumed his progress when making his handicap debut in a novice contest at Wetherby on Boxing Day where Hamilton won the first three races on the card for the Walford stable. Chasingouttheblues did well to get his nose in front—that's all he had to spare—as he was carried left on the run-in by runner-up Jazz King. He followed up with another narrow success in a handicap at Ayr in January when he was stepped up to three miles for the first time. As expected, he benefited from the longer trip and again showed a likeable attitude to come out on top, edging ahead on the run-in to get the better of the favourite Gaillimh A Stor by a neck.

Chasingouttheblues made his next appearance in better handicap company, contesting a Pertemps Qualifier at Haydock on the day Hamilton had his big win on Battle Born Lad. Given he was badly hampered by a faller three out and still had plenty to do at the next, Chasingouttheblues did well to take third close home behind One Big Bang and Doddiethegreat, the latter going on to win the Pertemps Final at Cheltenham. He disappointed in a big field at Uttoxeter next time when his stable was going less well, but Chasingouttheblues ended his campaign on a positive note at Ayr when a staying-on sixth to Billy Boi Blue, though the good ground made it an insufficient test for Chasingouttheblues who ideally needs it softer. Placed on all four of his starts in Irish points, Chasingouttheblues has a good attitude and is a thorough stayer so appeals as the sort who should take to fences if tried. **Mark Walford**

Conclusion: *Proved himself a likeable type with a productive first season under Rules, winning three times over hurdles, and will win more races given a sufficient test of stamina*

Simon Walker (Chasingouttheblues): *"Chasingouttheblues will hopefully be doing just that this winter. He won three of his seven starts over hurdles last season, impressing as a dogged stayer with a likeable attitude, and is just the type to make an even better chaser given he was placed on all four starts in Irish points and has enough physical scope to believe he should take to the larger obstacles. He's likely to come into his own when stamina is at a premium."*

Conman John (Ire)   b90

5 br.g. Malinas (Ger) – Shanclough (Ire) (Oscar (Ire))
2024/25 b16.9d² b18.8d⁵ May 2

Myretown, carrying the red silks of Carron Wymer that came to prominence due to the exploits of Ahoy Senor, justified his inclusion among last season's *Fifty* by winning three races during his first campaign over fences, most notably the Ultima Handicap Chase at the Cheltenham Festival. Myretown was providing trainer Lucinda Russell with a third win in the Ultima in the last four years, following back-to-back victories for Corach Rambler in 2022 and 2023, and his progressive profile ensures he remains one to follow. He's not the only promising type Wymer and Russell—who has been joined on the training licence by Michael Scudamore, son of her partner Peter—have on their hands, however, as Conman John also appeals as one to be positive about.

Conman John, a €31,000 purchase as a three-year-old, was picked up by his current connections for £170,000 after winning a point by 20 lengths, emulating Ahoy Senor and Myretown who were both successful in that sphere. In keeping with that pair, Conman John was also beaten on his debut under Rules, but he shaped with promise despite failing to justify 11/8 favouritism at Newcastle in February. He had no answer to the impressive turn of foot found by Upon Tweed, who scooted eight and a half lengths clear at the end of a steadily-run race, but he stuck to his task to prove best of the rest.

Conman John underlined that promise when finishing fifth in a much more competitive bumper over an extra couple of furlongs at the Punchestown Festival, shaping well to boot behind the exciting Soldier In Milan (who features among our Irish list). Conman John was beaten around 13 lengths but was probably unlucky not to finish a bit closer given he was left with a lot to do and was forced very wide on the turn for home before running on strongly. By noted stamina influence Malinas, Conman John's strength in the finish at Punchestown suggests he's likely to stay well and this expensive purchase from the pointing field should be capable of making his mark in northern novice hurdles this season before ultimately flourishing over fences. **Lucinda Russell & Michael Scudamore**

Conclusion: *Likely to excel in staying chases down the line but showed enough ability in bumpers to suggest he can win novice hurdles in the North*

Dedicated Hero (Ire) h128

6 b.g. Shirocco (Ger) – True Dedication (Ire) (Revoque (Ire))
2024/25 b16.2g* h20d³ h16.2s* h15.7s* h23.9s⁵ Apr 23

It seems certain that Dedicated Hero will be making more visits to Kelso this season. He's trained not far away but he's also unbeaten in three starts there so that's worth noting for any further appearances at his local track. Both his bumper wins came at Kelso, with the more important of them coming very early last season in the final of the Go North series which had been rescued from an abandoned Kelso card the previous March. A well-backed favourite, Dedicated Hero travelled well and won with a bit in hand.

After looking in need of the experience on his debut over hurdles when third on his return in a novice at Carlisle in the autumn, Dedicated Hero was back at Kelso for a maiden in December. He proved much the best, soon settling the issue after two out and winning with plenty in hand from Lost Frequencies who started at a shade of odds-on. Dedicated Hero looked capable of holding his own in better company and the following month he went to Haydock for the Rossington Main Novices' Hurdle, starting second favourite behind Dan Skelton's hot favourite Royal Infantry who had looked a good prospect in winning his first two starts over hurdles.

However, Royal Infantry proved a major let-down in fourth whereas Dedicated Hero showed plenty of improvement in what was an admittedly substandard renewal of a Grade 2 won by Jonbon three years earlier. He was value for more than the half-length he had to spare over Irish mare Cloonainra at the line as he found himself caught in a pocket at a crucial stage but rallied to lead soon after the last. Dedicated Hero was forced to miss an intended return to Kelso for the Premier Novices' Hurdle in March and instead faced a stiff task conceding weight all round in a three-mile listed novice at Perth the following month, over a full mile further than the Rossington Main. He saw out the much longer trip but could finish only fifth to the Willie Mullins-trained Kiss Will. The quite good-topped Dedicated Hero had finished third in both his Irish points, the first of which was won by future Grade 1 novice hurdle winner Romeo Coolio, and he looks the type to improve further when sent over fences. **Sandy Thomson**

Conclusion: *Progressed well in novice hurdles and his versatility will give connections plenty of options*

Derryhassen Paddy (left) showed a fine attitude when battling to win at Windsor

Derryhassen Paddy (Ire) h137

6 b.g. Arctic Cosmos (USA) – Kerrie Girl (Ire) (Golan (Ire))
2024/25 h19.9v* h24d* h24d³ Mar 14

Lucinda Russell's Kinross yard has developed into the most powerful jumps stable in the North in recent seasons, with its success built largely on buying chasing types out of Irish points. Ahoy Senor and the stable's two Grand National winners, One For Arthur and Corach Rambler, are all leading examples, and another with the potential to rank alongside those in the seasons to come is Derryhassen Paddy, a strong gelding who has chaser written all over him and is by St Leger winner Arctic Cosmos, already the sire of the stable's useful staying chaser Apple Away.

The winner of his sole start in Irish points in December 2023, Derryhassen Paddy made a successful debut for current connections in a bumper at Ayr a couple of months later, making all the running to come home seven lengths clear in a strung-out field in testing conditions. Last season, Derryhassen Paddy kept his unbeaten record for another couple of outings as he made a fine start over hurdles. After jumping fluently on his hurdles debut at Uttoxeter, he took on better rivals in the Berkshire Winter

Million Novices' Hurdle at Windsor in January. The five runners looked closely matched on form but Derryhassen Paddy, stepping up markedly in trip to three miles, was sent off the 2/1 favourite and came out on top, albeit very narrowly. Making most of the running, Derryhassen Paddy was headed by Honky Tonk Highway at the last but fought back tenaciously despite being short of room against the rail to force his nose in front on the line.

Derryhassen Paddy met with defeat for the first time in the Albert Bartlett Novices' Hurdle at the Cheltenham Festival, the race which had provided his trainer with her first Grade 1 success with Brindisi Breeze in 2012. But he produced his best effort yet to finish third behind Irish pair Jasmin de Vaux and The Big Westerner, his efforts in helping force a sound pace just telling in the closing stages. That hard race ruled him out of going for the Sefton at Aintree but, in any case, hurdling was always going to be a means to an end for Derryhassen Paddy who looks a smashing type for staying novice chases this season. He wears a tongue tie. **Lucinda Russell & Michael Scudamore**

Conclusion: *Winning pointer who kept his unbeaten record under Rules until finishing third in the Albert Bartlett at Cheltenham; very much the type to come into his own over fences*

Matt Brocklebank (Derryhassen Paddy): *"Lucinda Russell has already had significant success courtesy of Arctic Cosmos as a sire - the mare Apple Away landed the Grade 1 Sefton Novices' Hurdle at Aintree and a Listed chase at Perth - and she'll rightly have major hopes for this highly promising son of the 2010 St Leger winner. Everything about him suggests he will only come to fruition with time and distance, yet he still managed to win a bumper over two miles and remained unbeaten until finishing third in the Albert Bartlett Novices' Hurdle at Cheltenham. He's surely among the best staying novice chase prospect outside of Ireland."*

Diva Luna (Ire)   h129
6 b.m. Diamond Boy (Fr) – Longhouse Presents (Presenting)
2024/25 h16s² h20.3s* h16s² h16.8d³ h16.5g Apr 4

Diva Luna experienced something of a mixed campaign last term as she suffered a couple of short-price defeats, but she also offered a reminder of her class when third in the Dawn Run Mares' Novices' Hurdle at the Cheltenham Festival, and she remains one to be positive about with chasing in mind.

It was Diva Luna's bumper form in 2023/24 which accounted for her being sent off at very short odds for her hurdling debut at Lingfield in November. She had won both her starts in bumpers, notably the Grade 2 Nickel Coin for mares at the Grand National meeting. However, she was unable to uphold the form with fourth-placed Metkayina at Lingfield where her rival's jumping experience proved crucial. Stepping up to two and a half miles, Diva Luna got off the mark in convincing fashion in an uncompetitive contest at Cheltenham on New Year's Day, but she was turned over again at Sandown a few weeks later. Back at two miles, Diva Luna jumped fluently in the lead and showed improved form, but she simply bumped into a better rival in Castle Carrock who readily took her measure after the last.

That defeat at 2/9 didn't deter connections from having a crack at the Dawn Run at Cheltenham where Diva Luna fared best of the home team in finishing third of 23 in the largest field yet for the Grade 2 contest. Ridden with a bit more restraint but in the firing line throughout, Diva Luna led the field turning into the straight but was headed on the long run to the last and was ultimately beaten six and a half lengths by Air of Entitlement who overhauled the favourite Sixandahalf close to the line.

Diva Luna had more on her plate in the Top Novices' Hurdle at Aintree on her final start of the campaign, but that run can be ignored as she finished lame. A well-made mare who finished runner-up in her sole start in Irish points, Diva Luna has the background, demeanour and physique to take well to chasing. Encouragement can also be taken from her pedigree as she's out of a half-sister to smart Irish staying chaser Longhouse Poet. **Ben Pauling**

Conclusion: *Ran her best race over hurdles when third in the Dawn Run at the Cheltenham Festival and looks the type to do better still over fences*

George's Lad (Ire)   h126p

5 b.g. Order of St George (Ire) – Undecided Hall (Ire) (Saddlers' Hall (Ire))
2024/25 h18.5d⁵ h16d² h15.8s² h19.4d* h19.8d^F Mar 8

A horse doesn't necessarily have to complete a race to be credited with an improved performance. If the horse departs the race late enough in the contest for its finishing position and distance beaten to be estimated with a fair amount of confidence, it makes sense to rate the horse in question on where it would likely have finished, rather than ignore the performance completely. Last-flight faller George's Lad was one such example in the valuable novice handicap hurdle at Sandown in March which serves as the final of the EBF series.

George's Lad was keeping on in fourth at the time and likely to have finished in that position at worst had he not come down. In a dramatic finish, rather than one of the three who had been left clear, it was 33/1 shot Laurens Bay, who was back in seventh jumping the last and still with plenty to do, who conjured a storming run to collar the leading trio close home.

The performance continued the theme of run-by-run improvement from George's Lad who had shaped as if needing the outing on his hurdles debut at Exeter in October but built on that to finish second on his next two starts in an EBF qualifier at Kempton and a maiden at Huntingdon. His breakthrough came in a maiden later in January when stepping up nearly half a mile in trip at Doncaster. Notably strong in the market, George's Lad landed the odds under Harry Cobden with any amount in hand after leading on the bridle soon after the last. He was then sent off the 13/2 third choice in the market at Sandown where he gave the impression that he was suited by the even greater emphasis on stamina.

A strong, chasing type from the first crop of Gold Cup winner Order of St George, George's Lad is a half-brother to the fairly useful hurdler/fair chaser Will Sting who stayed two and a half miles, while his grandam was a sister to Irish Champion Hurdle winner Ned Kelly. Incidentally, he also came to grief at the last on his sole start in Irish points when in with every chance. He should take to chasing and can continue on his upward curve. **Emma Lavelle**

Conclusion: *Type to do well over fences having progressed with each run over hurdles; was set to make the frame in the EBF Final at Sandown when falling at the last*

Haiti Couleurs (Fr)   c152p

8 b.g. Dragon Dancer – Inchala (Fr) (Argument (Fr))
2024/25 c23.6d² c25g* c25.3d* h24.2s³ c29.9d* c29.2s* Apr 21

Haiti Couleurs looks a worthy ante-post favourite for the 2026 Grand National following a novice season where he was nothing short of a revelation over fences, showing all the qualities of an ideal Aintree candidate. His success reflected the better fortunes of the stable in general, with Rebecca Curtis sending out 20 winners in Britain during the season, matching a total she'd last reached in 2019/20. That was also the season of Lisnagar Oscar's win in the Stayers' Hurdle. Haiti Couleurs became a Festival winner himself—his trainer's sixth—but unlike the 50/1 shock pulled off by Lisnagar Oscar, Haiti Couleurs was sent off one of the 7/2 joint-favourites for the National Hunt Novices' Chase. The race has changed since the yard's Teaforthree won it in 2012—it's a bit shorter, for one thing, while the latest edition was the first run as a handicap open to professional jockeys—but it remains a test of stamina and jumping and Haiti Couleurs handled it much the best. He jumped accurately up with the pace and, having been left clear at the second last, saw things out well to win in straightforward fashion by four and a half lengths from Rock My Way.

Haiti Couleurs had already shown plenty of stamina over hurdles, winning his last two starts the previous season in the mud at Chepstow and Bangor. After finishing second on his chasing debut at Chepstow on his reappearance, Haiti Couleurs went on to win novice handicaps at Aintree and Cheltenham, both races which future Festival and Grand National winner Corach Rambler had also won three years earlier.

Haiti Couleurs forged clear in the Irish Grand National to cap an outstanding campaign

He then limbered up for the Festival with an encouraging third in a handicap hurdle at Newbury.

Haiti Couleurs' Festival success wasn't even the highlight of his season as he went on to follow up in the Irish Grand National where he improved again, putting up a smart performance. Travelling and jumping well again in a share of the lead, Sean Bowen sent him on four out and he stayed on well to win by three and a quarter lengths from the veteran 2022 Grand National runner-up Any Second Now. The well-made Haiti Couleurs, who acts on heavy ground but doesn't need the mud, is open to further improvement and will have his sights set on becoming the latest Irish Grand National winner to win at Aintree the following spring. **Rebecca Curtis**

Conclusion: *Proved a revelation in his first season over fences, looking an ideal Aintree candidate following wins in the National Hunt Chase and Irish Grand National in the spring*

Idaho Sun (Ire)   b112

5 b.g. Idaho (Ire) – West Elite (Ire) (Westerner)
2024/25 b16.8s* b16d* b16.4d⁶ Mar 12

The latest Champion Bumper wasn't the truly-run race it usually is and that didn't suit Idaho Sun who has a staying pedigree and will be suited by greater tests of stamina over hurdles. Nonetheless, Idaho Sun's effort at the Festival, where he rallied well to finish sixth behind Bambino Fever, represented further improvement on his first two starts in bumpers, both of which he had won. Harry Fry gave him plenty of time between his races, with his debut coming at Newton Abbot at the end of October and his next start being in the valuable bumper at the Winter Millions meeting in January, with National Hunt racing making a welcome return to Windsor.

Idaho Sun had just a short head to spare on his debut at Newton Abbot but there was a lot to like about the way he overcame his inexperience to edge ahead close home from the Dan Skelton-trained favourite Supreme Malinas after the third, Gentleman Toboot, had shaped like the winner for a long way. That race worked out well, with both placed horses having won by the time Idaho Sun went to Windsor where Supreme Malinas, successful in a listed mares' race at Huntingdon, was again one of his rivals. However, she was beaten further in third this time as Idaho Sun showed some improvement, still looking a little rough around the edges but ultimately keeping on well to win by three lengths from Kocktail Bleu.

The good-topped Idaho Sun comes from the first crop of Irish Derby runner-up Idaho whose wins included the Great Voltigeur and the Hardwicke Stakes and who had form up to two miles. A €60,000 three-year-old, he's the only runner so far for his unraced dam West Elite, a half-sister to the useful if unreliable Oscar Elite, a winner of the Reynoldstown Novices' Chase. Idaho Sun's grandam was a half-sister to the surprise 2014 Cheltenham Gold Cup winner Lord Windermere. **Harry Fry**

Conclusion: *Staying type who nonetheless had the speed to win his first two bumpers on flat tracks before keeping on well in sixth in the Champion Bumper; should do well in novice hurdles*

Jagwar (Fr)　　　　　　　　　　　　c150p

6 b.g. Karaktar (Ire) – Quizas Jolie (Fr) (Video Rock (Fr))
2024/25 c19.4d* c20.3s* c20s³ c20.6s* c20.6d* Mar 13

The Timeform Novices' Handicap Chase on Festival Trials Day has proved a significant pointer to the big meeting in March and the latest winner, Jagwar, enhanced that record by justifying favouritism in the TrustATrader Plate. Jagwar was emulating Simply The Betts who won both contests in 2020, while Mister Whitaker (2018 novice handicap chase) and Stage Star (2023 Turners Novices' Chase) have also done the Trials Day-Festival double in recent years. Stage Star went on to win the Paddy Power Gold Cup on his reappearance the following season, and that prestigious handicap appeals as a suitable option for Jagwar, though graded races could well be on his agenda before long given the remarkable progress he made during his novice campaign.

A narrow victory in a Carlisle novice was Jagwar's only win from five starts over hurdles for Oliver Greenall and Josh Guerriero in the previous campaign, but as a tall, lengthy type he always had the raw materials to make a better chaser. Plenty of punters were certainly expecting him to improve for the switch to fences as he was sent off a strong evens favourite for a handicap chase at Wetherby in October and he justified that support with a cosier victory than the half-length margin might suggest. He then had little trouble following up in a similar contest at Bangor where he readily quickened three lengths clear of chasing debutant Lowry's Bar who went on to win his next two starts and show smart form.

Jagwar endured his sole setback of the campaign when only third behind the promising Jingko Blue at Uttoxeter, though he would have finished runner-up and much closer to the winner had he not made a bad mistake at the final fence when only a couple of lengths down. Mistakes also threatened to be Jagwar's undoing in the TrustATrader Plate, for which he was sent off 3/1 favourite in much the most competitive race he's tackled, but it says plenty about his ability that he ultimately ran out a decisive two-and-three-quarter-length winner from well-backed second favourite Thecompanysergeant. He'd been much more fluent when producing a performance of style and substance in the Timeform on Trials Day, winning by two and a half lengths after tanking his way through the contest.

Described by Greenall as 'the biggest horse we've ever had', Jagwar has the scope to carry on progressing and is completely unexposed at staying trips having been campaigned exclusively around two and a half miles over fences. **Oliver Greenall & Josh Guerriero**

Conclusion: *Made giant strides during his first season over fences and signed off with victory in the TrustATrader Plate at Cheltenham; can make his mark in graded company when the time comes*

Jango Baie (Fr)   c155

6 b.g. Tiger Groom – Tenessee (Fr) (Kapgarde (Fr))
2024/25 c20.6d* c20v² c15.9d* c19.9g³ Apr 3

Winners of the Arkle Challenge Trophy at the Cheltenham Festival typically develop into leading contenders for the following season's Queen Mother Champion Chase, but it's hard to imagine that race will be on the agenda for Jango Baie; indeed, it wouldn't be a surprise were Jango Baie never to race in a two-mile chase again given how he shaped for much of the Arkle.

Jango Baie, dropping in trip following a novice chase win at Cheltenham and a runner-up effort in the Grade 1 Scilly Isles at Sandown at around two and a half miles, looked uncomfortable with the strong tempo in the Arkle and was outpaced in last at the top of the hill. The game looked up when he blundered at three out, but, having hit an in-running high of 300 on Betfair, Jango Baie started to engage top gear after the second last and, despite still being only fourth at the final fence and with a few lengths to find, he powered up the hill to claim the prize in a blanket finish.

Jango Baie (right) powered home to snatch victory from the jaws of defeat in the Arkle

That performance suggested he would relish a return to longer trips, though he failed to show improvement straight away in the two-and-a-half-mile Manifesto Novices' Chase at Aintree where he finished a close-up third, running to a similar level on Timeform's figures as in the Arkle. However, Jango Baie was the only runner in the nine-strong field that had competed at Cheltenham, and Timeform's reporter noted he looked a bit light in condition only 23 days after his Arkle exploits. A steady pace at Aintree also wouldn't have suited Jango Baie, who again proved notably strong after the final fence in the style of one capable of raising his game under more favourable circumstances. The feeling remains that a stronger pace at two and a half miles or perhaps an even sterner stamina test at three miles could draw a high-class performance from this lightly-raced chaser. **Nicky Henderson**

Conclusion: *Stormed home to gain an unlikely victory in the Arkle and looks capable of better form over longer trips*

Jesuila des Mottes (Fr)   h111

6 b.m. Voiladenuo (Fr) – Ouhetu des Mottes (Fr) (Ungaro (Ger))
2024/25 h21.2d h19.5d³ h20.4d³ h23.9d* Jan 18

The grey mare My Silver Lining has been a fine servant for Emma Lavelle's stable in staying handicap chases in recent seasons. She won the Classic Chase at Warwick early in 2024 before finishing placed in the Grand National Trial and Midlands Grand National later that season, and she was fourth in the latest renewal of the latter contest. My Silver Lining's regular jockey is James Best, also the son-in-law of the mare's owner Celia Djivanovic. Best should be able to look forward to further success in the yellow and black colours on another mare from the same stable judged on Jesuila des Mottes' win at Taunton on her final start last season.

Jesuila des Mottes remains lightly raced after only one start in bumpers and four over hurdles. As in her bumper, she looked in need of the experience on her debut over hurdles at Ludlow but there was more encouragement from her next couple of runs when third in mares' maidens at Lingfield and Southwell. Her form improved again when she was stepped up to three miles at Taunton in January for her handicap debut in a novice contest. The form of her previous race was beginning to work out well and, belying market weakness which had her starting at 22/1, she relished the longer trip. Produced by Best to lead before two out, Jesuila des Mottes kept on well to beat favourite Badbury Rings by a length and three quarters with a dozen lengths back to the third. She took the scalp of a progressive rival there as the runner-up went on to win his next two starts.

Jesuila des Mottes isn't by one of the better-known French jumps sires on this side of the Channel. Voiladenuo has had a handful of winners in Britain, though, and was a talented jumper himself in France, showing very smart form over hurdles, including winning a Group 2 at Auteuil, as well as winning over fences. While Jesuila des Mottes' dam was less talented, she too had a successful jumping career. Having won three bumpers in France, she joined the late Edward O'Grady in Ireland, winning a maiden hurdle at Sligo, before rejoining her original connections in France where she won twice more over hurdles. Jesuila des Mottes has worn a tongue tie for her last three starts. **Emma Lavelle**

Conclusion: *French non-thoroughbred mare who showed improved form when stepped up to three miles in a light hurdles campaign and is open to further progress*

Job (Fr)   h111p

6 b.g. Coastal Path – Cavalerie (Fr) (Network (Ger))
2024/25 h19.7d³ h19.9d⁴ h24.3d* h24.2d² Jan 15

Owner Robert Kirkland's red colours have been carried with distinction by high-class chaser Grey Dawning in recent seasons, winner of the Turners Novices' Chase at the

Cheltenham Festival in 2024 and runner-up last season in the Betfair Chase at Haydock and the Bowl Chase at Aintree. Most of the owner's jumpers are with Dan Skelton, but Kirkland also has horses with Toby Lawes who looks to have a promising novice chaser for the season ahead with Job. It's highly unlikely he'll reach the same heights as Grey Dawning, but he does look the type to take well to fences, particularly when stamina is at a premium.

Job, who has worn a hood for all his starts, showed a little ability in a couple of bumpers but fared better when sent over hurdles last season, particularly when stepped up to three miles. His first two runs were at shorter, and while there was more encouragement from his third in a novice at Wetherby on his reappearance in October, he went backwards from that when only fourth of five finishers in a maiden at Uttoxeter the following month. But he confirmed the promise of his hurdling debut when stepped up in trip for his handicap debut at Southwell in December, evidently relishing the greater test of stamina. Making the running as usual, Job briefly looked in trouble when headed on the home turn by Magical Arthur, who had won three of his last four starts, but Job was more fluent at the final flight and was driven out to win by a length and a quarter, completing a treble on the card for his jockey Harry Bannister.

Job was seen out only once more, improving again in defeat in a better race at Newbury in January. Jumping well in front, Job impressed with his attitude when headed by eventual winner Keable on the home turn as he stuck to his task in going down by three and a half lengths. A good-topped son of Coastal Path whose offspring have done well for Willie Mullins in particular—Asterion Forlonge, Franco de Port and Bacardys to name but three—Job was fourth on his sole start in Irish points before joining current connections. He's likely to do better still as a chaser. **Toby Lawes**

Conclusion: *Proved suited by a test of stamina over hurdles and looks the type to improve further as a chaser*

Juby Ball (Fr) h124p

6 b.g. Nom de d'La (Fr) – Voix de Montot (Fr) (Voix du Nord (Fr))
2024/25 h15.8v* h16v* Feb 9

The bumper on Sandown's Scilly Isles Novices' Chase card in February 2024 turned out to be a good one featuring some useful future hurdlers. The first five all went on to win over hurdles last season with winner Sixmilebridge proving the best of them, completing a hat-trick when landing the Classic Novices' Hurdle at Cheltenham on Trials Day. Another to do well was Wellington Arch who finished fourth at Sandown; he ended last season beating a big field in a premier handicap at Aintree and is included among our *Fifty*. Juby Ball, who caught the eye in finishing second at Sandown, was less highly tried over hurdles than either of those two, but he won both his starts during the winter to maintain a very positive profile and looks likely to progress further with more racing, probably over fences.

Juby Ball was already proven in very testing conditions having made a successful debut in a bumper for conditional jockeys and amateur riders at Ffos Las prior to his run at Sandown which was on going no worse than good to soft. His two runs over hurdles, though, were both back on heavy ground. After 11 months off, he reappeared at Ffos Las in January in a maiden hurdle and, despite the conditions and his own stout pedigree, he showed no lack of speed in travelling best of all through the race and then quickening clear when produced to lead at the final flight. He won by four lengths from Lud'or who won his next start, while Juby Ball followed up at Chepstow in a very uncompetitive novice which he won with plenty in hand by six lengths, giving the impression that his starts so far have only scratched the surface of his ability.

Raced only at two miles, Juby Ball is bred to stay a good deal further. His sire Nom de D'la, a fairly useful hurdler/chaser in France, is a brother to better-known French sire Nickname who was responsible for the likes of Cyrname and Frodon. Nom de D'la has had only a handful of winners in Britain to date, one of the others being the aforementioned Lud'or. Younger brother Kaiser Ball made a successful debut for Willie Mullins in a bumper at Fairyhouse in February, while elder half-brother Fifty Ball was second in the Betfair Hurdle but later stayed beyond three miles. **Evan Williams**

Conclusion: *Winner of three of his four starts, including both over hurdles, and remains capable of better; should be suited by longer trips*

Jupiter des Bordes (Fr) c105

6 b.g. Buck's Boum (Fr) – Bossa Nova (Fr) (Network (Ger))
2024/25 h20.9v h18.9d^3 h19.4v^{ur} c17.9v^4 c20d^3 c20s^3 c20s^4 c21.6g^2 Apr 11

Jupiter des Bordes was a mid-season addition to Richard Hobson's string from France, and while he didn't manage to win over fences for his new stable, he showed enough to suggest that there are races to be won with him this season, most likely when he is stepped up in trip. He had winning form over hurdles for his previous trainer, Augustin de Boisbrunet, having won at long odds at La Teste in May 2024 when returning from a lengthy absence after making his debut for another yard. After three more runs over hurdles, which yielded a third place in a handicap at Moulins, Jupiter des Bordes finished fourth on his chasing debut at Lignieres in November on his final start in France.

Jupiter des Bordes made the frame in all four of his starts in handicap chases in Britain after the turn of the year. He wasn't at his best when fourth at Uttoxeter in the third of those but otherwise showed a fair level of form which was on a par with the best of his hurdles form in France. He twice finished third at Warwick and after Uttoxeter soon got back on track when runner-up at Fontwell in April. He didn't travel particularly smoothly and got outpaced going to the last but kept on to finish two and a half lengths behind Sherborne. That performance was very much in keeping with earlier impressions that Jupiter des Bordes is essentially a stayer. Raced mainly at distances around two and a half miles to date, he shapes as though he will be suited by three miles.

His breeding backs that up as he's by Buck's Boum, a half-brother to Big Buck's. His standout jumper this side of the Channel is dual Cheltenham Gold Cup winner Al Boum Photo. Jupiter des Bordes has worn a tongue tie for all his races, and he was tried in cheekpieces a couple of times in France. **Richard Hobson**

Conclusion: *French import who will be suited by more of a stamina test than he's faced so far; still a novice over fences so connections will have options*

Kabral du Mathan (Fr) h140
5 b.g. Pastorius (Ger) – Nasthazya (Fr) (Rochesson (Fr))
2024/25 h16d* h15.7d² h16d² h16d² Apr 12

Paul Nicholls lost several high-profile horses to other yards over the summer and it's not hard to see why he picked out Kabral du Mathan as one he'll miss in particular. The five-year-old has been a model of consistency in his brief career so far, winning his first three starts over hurdles—his debut came in France—before finishing runner-up in

Kabral du Mathan (near side) was only narrowly denied in a thrilling finish to the Scottish Champion Hurdle

three valuable handicap hurdles to end last season. Nicholls would surely have found more winning opportunities for Kabral du Mathan, whom he had earmarked to go chasing this season, but that will now be the task of his new trainer Dan Skelton.

Kabral du Mathan went into handicaps last season with just two runs behind him in juvenile hurdles. He made a winning debut for Arnaud Chaille-Chaille at Clairefontaine and then impressed on his first start for Nicholls when readily winning a slowly-run edition of the Chatteris Fen Juvenile Hurdle at Huntingdon. What Nicholls described as 'a little problem' meant he wasn't seen again that season, but when he did reappear in a conditional jockeys' handicap at Kempton in November, he made a mockery of his opening mark to win impressively by just under five lengths.

Although he was weak in the market, Kabral du Mathan only narrowly failed to keep his unbeaten record from an 8 lb higher mark in the Ladbrokes Hurdle at Ascot just before Christmas, travelling well and keeping on to go down by a short head to Fiercely Proud after Secret Squirrel's fall at the last had left the pair a long way clear. Kabral du Mathan faced another 8 lb hike in the weights in the following month's Sovereign Handicap Hurdle at Windsor where he and Secret Squirrel were the first two in the betting. They duly finished first and second with Kabral du Mathan staying on to take second on the line, two lengths behind the winner to whom he was conceding almost a stone. What turned out to be Kabral du Mathan's final start for Nicholls came in the Scottish Champion Hurdle where he led between the final two flights before going down by a neck to Cracking Rhapsody. The good-topped Kabral du Mathan, who wears a tongue tie (he also wore a hood in France) should do at least as well over fences and will stay further than two miles. **Dan Skelton**

Conclusion: *Strong-travelling type who proved a model of consistency over hurdles and, having swapped one top stable for another over the summer, looks a novice chaser to follow*

Kepler's Law   h125
6 b.g. Jack Hobbs – Wee Orbit (Kayf Tara)
2024/25 h20g³ h22g³ h20.5v* h19.8d Mar 8

The field for the EBF Betfair 'National Hunt' Novices' Handicap Hurdle Final at Sandown in March was a good one on looks and plenty of them have long-term potential as chasers. Included among those is George's Lad, a fellow member of our *Fifty*, who was a faller at the last, while another is Kepler's Law who was only eighth of the ten finishers but had excuses in what was much the most competitive race of his short career to date. A bit keener than ideal despite the good pace, a return to more prominent tactics didn't suit given how the race was run, and he was on the retreat when hampered by George's Lad's late fall.

Kepler's Law had just three runs in novices for Laura Morgan prior to Sandown. His jumping was less than polished on his first couple of starts, but he managed to finish third both times, behind the impressive Mister Meggit at Aintree and the prolific winner Skyjack Hijack at Newcastle. By January, though, his yard was in better form, and he ran out an emphatic winner at Leicester. Ridden more patiently under much more testing conditions than for his first couple of starts, Kepler's Law made headway on the bridle to lead on the approach to two out and then drew clear to win by 30 lengths from the favourite Barlovento.

The rangy Kepler's Law, who looks very much the type to take to fences, is one of the best jumpers from the early crops of Irish Derby winner Jack Hobbs. His unraced dam is out of Wee Dinns, a useful winner over hurdles at short of two and a half miles for the Pipe stable. Kepler's Law, who won his only Irish point by a dozen lengths, has joined Christian Williams since last season and his new stable could well have a useful novice chaser on its hands. **Christian Williams**

Conclusion: *Chaser on looks who came up short in the EBF Final at Sandown but made a very good impression at Leicester the time before and still has few miles on the clock*

Kingston Queen (Ire) b103

5 gr.m. Kingston Hill – Competitive Affair (Ire) (Presenting)
2024/25 b16d³ b17.7s² b16.8d* b16.6d* b17g³ Apr 3

Aintree's Nickel Coin Mares' Bumper is often a good source of winners over hurdles for the following season and the 2024 renewal, in which Diva Luna beat Jubilee Alpha, was no exception. All bar two of the 14 fillies and mares from that contest who went on to run over hurdles last season were successful, the first two being among four to earn black type. The latest renewal might not prove quite as strong and the Irish-trained winner Seo Linn has more of a Flat profile, but that's not to say there weren't any good jumping prospects among the beaten horses, and third-placed Kingston Queen makes as much appeal as any over hurdles this term.

While the winner justified strong support, Kingston Queen was sent off at 14/1, though her form made her one of the leading home-trained contenders. Having her first start since January, Kingston Queen ran at least as well as previously and stuck to her task well after disputing the lead for much of the way, keeping on to be beaten just over two lengths. Placed on her first two starts at Chepstow and Plumpton and looking a stayer when beaten a neck at the latter track, Kingston Queen got off the mark against her own sex at Sedgefield on Boxing Day where she made all the running to win convincingly. Even so, she looked to have something to find in listed company at Market Rasen the following month, but her conditional rider Gearoid Harney, unable to claim this time, pulled off the same tactics and she held on to score by a neck from

Alan King's dual winner Charisma Cat with Dream Shadow back in third. The placed horses then gave that form a boost by filling the first two positions in a listed contest at Sandown in March.

The workmanlike Kingston Queen is a daughter of St Leger winner Kingston Hill and was bought for £80,000 at the Cheltenham Festival Sale in 2024 shortly after winning her only start in Irish points. She's a first winner for her dam, an unraced sister to Competitive Edge whose career-best effort came when showing smart form to finish runner-up in the valuable Guinness Handicap Chase over two and a half miles at the Punchestown Festival. This is also the family of useful Irish chaser Portrait King, a thorough stayer whose wins included the Eider Chase. **David Pipe**

Conclusion: *Winning pointer who progressed in her bumpers to finish third at Aintree and looks set for a bright future over jumps*

Last Rodeo (Ire) h111p

5 br.g. Malinas (Ger) – Western Cowgirl (Ire) (Westerner)
2024/25 h15.8s⁴ h16.5s³ h19.5s* Feb 20

Christian Williams has developed an enviable record in the sport's prestigious and valuable staying handicap chases and has won two editions of the Scottish Grand National as well as the 2019 Welsh Grand National and 2023 Bet365 Gold Cup. Last Rodeo is another in the stable who looks likely to come into his own in staying chases down the line as he's by noted stamina influence Malinas and is a brother to Malina Girl, a useful chaser who won the 2023 Ulster National over nearly three miles and five furlongs.

Given his stout pedigree and his stable's tendency to bring horses along slowly, it bodes well for Last Rodeo's prospects that he showed so much potential in maiden and novice hurdles, even managing to win on his final start of the campaign at Lingfield in February. Last Rodeo, who had finished fourth on his only start in an Irish point, was in need of the experience when a distant fourth on his hurdling debut at Ludlow in December, but he stepped up on that when third at Taunton the following month, keeping on in encouraging fashion in a race that would have placed far too much emphasis on speed.

A step up in trip helped Last Rodeo progress again at Lingfield where he was in command crossing the last and forged further clear up the run-in to score by nine lengths. The bare form is probably only fair, but such is the improvement that Last Rodeo has made with each start that he looks likely to develop into something much better in time. **Christian Williams**

Conclusion: *Has a stout pedigree so it is encouraging that he proved forward enough to win a novice hurdle; should carry on progressing and is one to note in handicaps*

Le Tiep's Sacre (Fr)   h112p

4 b.g. It's Gino (Ger) – Sacree Tiepy (Fr) (Ungaro (Ger))
2024/25 b11.9g² h17.9s³ h16s³ h17.7d* Mar 6

The weight-for-age allowance that four-year-old chasers receive from older horses is too generous, in Timeform's view, and was exploited on a number of occasions last season. Between the start of the jumps season and the turn of the year, a total of eight handicap chases were won by four-year-olds, and those winners came from only 38 representatives at a highly creditable strike rate of 21.1%.

One who could take advantage of the allowance should connections make the quick switch to chasing is the imposing French recruit Le Tiep's Sacre. Placed on both outings for David Cottin, Le Tiep's Sacre was purchased privately for €150,000 and sent to Gary and Josh Moore. It briefly looked like he was going to make a successful British debut at Sandown in February when he edged his way into the lead approaching the final flight, but a blunder perhaps exposed a lack of fitness on his first start for nearly four months, and he faded into third. That was still an encouraging start for his new connections, however, and Le Tiep's Sacre confirmed that promise when turning over the odds-on favourite, Walk On High, at Fontwell three weeks later. Le Tiep's Sacre understandably still looked raw up against a rival twice his age, but he found plenty to forge three and a quarter lengths clear of Walk On High who in turn was nine and a half lengths clear of the third, The Long Walk. That performance looks a lot better now than it did at the time as Walk On High has won both subsequent starts, while The Long Walk took a big step forward when a wide-margin winner of a maiden hurdle at Warwick.

Le Tiep's Sacre has not been seen since that victory in March but appeals as a likely improver and is one to note when he returns. He dwarfed Walk On High at Fontwell and, given he's out of a multiple winner in cross-country chases, has the hallmarks of one who will thrive over fences. **Gary & Josh Moore**

Conclusion: *French recruit who looked raw but produced a likeable performance when forging clear to win a Fontwell maiden that has proved a strong piece of form; could exploit a generous weight-for-age allowance if making the quick switch to chasing*

Lulamba (Fr)   h150p

4 b.g. Nirvana du Berlais (Fr) – Ejland (Fr) (Vision d'Etat (Fr))
2024/25 h17.9s* h15.7d* h16.8d² h16d* May 3

Let's hope Lulamba enjoys more luck in his first season over fences than the same connections' Sir Gino did. The top British-trained juvenile hurdler the season before, the hugely exciting Sir Gino kept his unbeaten record with a superb debut over fences in the Wayward Lad Novices' Chase at Kempton on Boxing Day only to miss

Lulamba (left) was only narrowly denied at Cheltenham but gained revenge at Punchestown

the rest of the campaign with an injury which looks set to keep him out of action for a while yet.

Awaiting Sir Gino's return, Nicky Henderson and owners Joe and Marie Donnelly have another exciting prospect in Lulamba who is set for a similar early switch to fences after also proving himself a top juvenile hurdler. Like Sir Gino, Lulamba won his only start at Auteuil before joining current connections. In Lulamba's case that was a contest for unraced non-thoroughbreds which he won by five lengths in October for Arnaud Chaille-Chaille. Lulamba made his British debut in a juvenile at Ascot in January against another notable French import in Mondo Man, though he had a very different background as a smart Flat performer who had finished fifth in the Prix du Jockey Club. Lulamba's defeat of Mondo Man, after leading on the bridle between the final two flights, was all the more impressive considering he was conceding the runner-up 10 lb, and he quickened clear to win with plenty in hand by three and a half lengths.

That performance made Lulamba much the most interesting rival to form pick East India Dock in the Triumph Hurdle, and while he looked to have done the hard work in edging ahead of that rival on the run-in, both were collared late on as hurdling newcomer Poniros got up to win by a neck at 100/1. That shock result did nothing to alter the fact that Lulamba looked the best long-term prospect in the Triumph field and he wasted no time in proving as much by turning the tables on the winner with a four-length success in the Champion Four Year Old Hurdle at Punchestown. This time, it was Lulamba who played his hand later and he was already getting on top when producing a more fluent jump than his rival at the final flight to seal matters. A well-made gelding from the first crop of Nirvana du Berlais, who was himself a smart juvenile hurdler in France, Lulamba should do at least as well switched to fences. **Nicky Henderson**

Conclusion: *Beaten by a shock winner in the Triumph Hurdle but quickly put the record straight at Punchestown and is an exciting prospect for chasing*

Miami Magic (Ire)   h132

6 ch.g. Leading Light (Ire) – Rose de Beaufai (Fr) (Solon (Ger))
2024/25 b17d² h16g* h16d* h17s² h16s² h20g Apr 5

Victories at two miles around sharp tracks like Fakenham and Kempton would suggest speed is a horse's forte. However, that's unlikely to be the case with Miami Magic who is expected to build on the solid foundations he laid at two miles during his novice hurdle campaign and truly flourish when presented with stiffer tests of stamina over fences.

Miami Magic, a half-brother to West Wales National winner Pobbles Bay, was successful on his third appearance in points for Dale Peters in March 2024 and then made an encouraging start under Rules a couple of months later when only narrowly denied in an Aintree bumper, with his trainer again in the saddle. Miami Magic was in the care of Stuart Edmunds by the time he made his hurdling debut at Fakenham in the autumn, and he built on his bumper promise to run out an emphatic ten-length winner under Charlie Hammond, showing an encouraging amount of speed given his pointing background and the fact his most talented sibling, Pobbles Bay, was such a strong stayer. Another wide-margin win, this time in a Kempton novice, earned Miami Magic a crack at the Grade 1 Formby Novices' Hurdle at Aintree on Boxing Day and, while visibility was limited, the result suggests he acquitted himself with great credit. He lost his unbeaten record over hurdles, but, in getting to within two and a quarter lengths of evens favourite Potters Charm, Miami Magic registered an improved Timeform rating and enhanced his reputation.

That reputation remains intact despite two further defeats. He ran another fine race when finding only Tripoli Flyer, one of the previous season's leading bumper performers, too strong in the Dovecote Novices' Hurdle at Kempton and he then had excuses when only seventh in the Mersey Novices' Hurdle at Aintree. The fact Miami

Magic was sent off the 5/2 favourite for a Grade 1 on his first attempt at two and a half miles underlines how he'd been shaping like a step up in trip would suit, but little went right at Aintree where he was soon on the back foot after blowing the standing start, pulled too hard and made a bad mistake at the final flight to exacerbate the distance beaten. He remains likely to appreciate at least two and a half miles under more favourable circumstances and, given he's a strong, chasing type in appearance, has the scope to progress over fences. **Stuart Edmunds**

Conclusion: *Finished runner-up in a Grade 1 novice during a successful first season over hurdles and looks the type to take well to chasing; should stay at least two and a half miles*

Mydaddypaddy (Ire)   b109p
4 b.g. Walk In The Park (Ire) – Debdebdeb (Teofilo (Ire))
2024/25 b15.8d* Mar 2

Not many horses manage to win on the Flat and over both hurdles and fences, but the mare Debdebdeb did just that. She was a talented all-rounder and showed useful form in all three disciplines. On the Flat, she won four races for Andrew Balding at up to a mile and three quarters before being sold to go jumping at the end of her four-year-old season. Her first win over hurdles came for Donald McCain before she moved on to Dan Skelton, for whom she won a second race over hurdles, picked up some black type from finishing second in a listed mares' handicap at Cheltenham and ended her career by winning two of her three starts over fences.

As a broodmare, Debdebdeb's first date was with 2000 Guineas and Derby winner Camelot, resulting in the useful Flat stayer Dillian. But reflecting her own dual-purpose racing career, she subsequently produced a foal to top jumping sire Walk In The Park and looks to have a very promising future jumper with the result of that mating being impressive Huntingdon bumper winner Mydaddypaddy. Ridden by Harry Skelton, who had partnered Debdebdeb to all three of her wins for the yard, Mydaddypaddy clearly came with something of a reputation and was sent off the 15/8 favourite for his debut.

He could hardly have won in more taking style having been dropped out last of all for much of the way. But towards the end of the back straight, Mydaddypaddy quickly began to pass horses on the bridle out wide and was still travelling strongly when produced to lead entering the straight. From that point, it was a one-horse race, with Mydaddypaddy readily quickening clear once shaken up to pull 11 lengths clear. That may have been a thin race, but that doesn't alter the fact that the tall, useful-looking Mydaddypaddy will be a most exciting prospect for novice hurdles. **Dan Skelton**

Conclusion: *Impressed with the way he cruised from last to first before pulling clear on his debut in a Huntingdon bumper and can take high rank in novice hurdles*

TIMEFORM'S FIFTY TO FOLLOW 2025/26 | 33

David Ord (Mydaddypaddy): *"He might have seen the trainers' title slip through his fingers on the final day of the last two seasons, but Dan Skelton goes into the new campaign with his largest ever string and with a host of exciting young prospects. Among those is Mydaddypaddy who looked something out of the ordinary when winning a Huntingdon bumper in March, making an eye-catching move from the rear turning in and then quickening clear of his rivals in a matter of strides. He's the sort to run up a sequence over hurdles before his sights are raised."*

Myretown (Ire) c142p
8 b.g. Dylan Thomas (Ire) – Miss Platinum (Ire) (Oscar (Ire))
2024/25 c16.4d⁵ c19.4s* c24.2dᶠ c23.4s* c25d* Mar 11

Having won back-to-back renewals of the Ultima Handicap Chase at the Cheltenham Festival with Corach Rambler, who went on to win the Grand National after the second of those wins in 2023, Lucinda Russell landed the Ultima again last season with the progressive Myretown who also looks to have even bigger days ahead of him over

Myretown proved well ahead of his mark in the Ultima Handicap Chase at Cheltenham

fences. As an eight-year-old novice at the foot of the weights, Myretown had a very similar profile to Corach Rambler when he won the Ultima for the first time.

As a youngster, Myretown had a lengthy spell on the sidelines after his sole outing in bumpers. He had just three runs over hurdles, falling on the second occasion but impressively winning a maiden at Kelso in the spring of 2024 when looking an exciting chasing prospect. After making his debut over fences at Newbury in the autumn over an inadequate two miles, Myretown soon made into a useful chaser, winning all three of his remaining completed starts. He had just one other finisher to beat at Wetherby on Boxing Day but fell three out at Windsor next time when set to play a part in the finish. On the whole, though, Myretown impressed with his jumping and was very good again in that department at Kelso in February when easily accounting for another small field in a Timeform-sponsored novice handicap. That was a far cry from the maximum field he faced in the Ultima but there was no lack of confidence in his chances at Cheltenham as he was gambled on and started the 13/2 favourite. With Myretown's usual rider Derek Fox opting to partner stablemate Whistle Stop Tour instead, Myretown provided the previous season's champion conditional Patrick Wadge with his first Festival winner. Jumping superbly for the most part, Myretown winged the last and bounded clear up the run-in to beat fellow novice The Changing Man by 11 lengths in the manner of a chaser well ahead of his mark.

A strong gelding, Myretown is by the same sire, Dylan Thomas, as his high-class stablemate Ahoy Senor who runs in the same colours. Like many of the stable's best chasers, Myretown was bought out of Irish points where he won at the second attempt after falling on his debut. He can go on improving and will take plenty of catching again in his second season over fences. **Lucinda Russell & Michael Scudamore**

Conclusion: *Front runner who is open to further improvement over fences after making a mockery of his mark in the Ultima*

No Drama This End (Ire)　　　　　　　　　　b109
5 gr.g. Walk In The Park (Ire) – La Segnora (Fr) (Turgeon (USA))
2024/25 b16s* b16.4d Mar 12

Paul Nicholls finished third in the latest trainers' championship and sent out his 50th Cheltenham Festival winner in March but other statistics show the 14-time champion didn't have the best of seasons by his very high standards. For the first time this century, Nicholls' strike-rate fell below 20%, while a total of 99 winners was only the third time since the 1999/2000 season that he hadn't reached a century of winners; the other occasions were in the seasons hit by foot-and-mouth disease and Covid. But with that Festival winner Caldwell Potter going on to win the Mildmay Novices' Chase at Aintree and stablemate Kalif du Berlais winning the Maghull Novices' Chase at the same meeting, the stable still has a promising team of younger horses coming through.

Another such horse is No Drama This End whose colours, those of part-owners Chris and Giles Barber, were formerly those of their late father Paul who launched Nicholls' career and was the owner of two of his Gold Cup winners See More Business and Denman. In his speech at Paul Barber's funeral in 2023, Nicholls vowed to reach the milestone of 4,000 winners in tribute to his former boss, a target he may well be close to by the end of the current season. No Drama This End moved Nicholls one step closer to that landmark by making a winning debut in a bumper at Warwick on New Year's Eve. Dan Skelton's newcomer Keops des Bordes was sent off the short-priced favourite but No Drama This End was very well backed against him and looked a good prospect in beating him impressively, quickening clear after leading entering the straight to win by three and a half lengths. On his only other start, No Drama This End acquitted himself well when mid-division in the Champion Bumper at Cheltenham considering the steadier than usual pace for that contest wouldn't have played to his strengths.

The useful-looking No Drama This End was bought for £160,000 after easily winning his sole start in points. By Walk In The Park, also sire of the stable's exciting novice chase prospect Regent's Stroll, No Drama This End is a brother to three winners out of La Segnora, a Group 1 winner over hurdles in France in the Grand Prix d'Automne and the winner of France's most prestigious handicap chase, the Prix du President de la Republique. **Paul Nicholls**

Conclusion: *Winning pointer who impressed on bumper debut before running at the Festival; looks the type to do well in novice hurdles given more of a test of stamina*

Our Boy Stan b93

4 b.g. Kapgarde (Fr) – Whoops A Daisy (Definite Article)
2024/25 b16.8s² b16s* Feb 22

The listed bumper at Cheltenham on New Year's Day for horses who have literally just turned four is effectively the season's championship race as far as junior bumpers are concerned. As a concession to the age of the participants, the race had previously been run at around a mile and three quarters, but the 2025 edition was the first run over a full bumper trip and, taking place on the New Course, is actually a little further than the Champion Bumper run on the Old Course at the Festival. It was won by 16/1 shot Precious Metal who provided Henrietta Knight with her biggest success since she came out of retirement. However, it was Caballero Cliff, fourth at 50/1, who fared best subsequently, excelling himself at three times those odds to fill the same position in the Champion Bumper and proving the best of the British.

Our Boy Stan built on his debut promise when a game winner at Kempton

One of the best jumping prospects in the field, though, was Our Boy Stan, one of four making his debut and bidding to become only the second horse to win it first time out. Trained by Ben Pauling, successful two years previously with Fiercely Proud who won last season's Ladbrokes Hurdle at Ascot, Our Boy Stan was weak in the market but shaped very promisingly in staying on for second, two lengths behind the winner. The following month at Kempton, Our Boy Stan showed battling qualities to go one better in a steadily-run six-runner contest. Main market rival Moneygarrow, a year older and himself runner-up in a listed contest at Ascot on his previous start, gave Our Boy Stan most to do, but Our Boy Stan kept on well when joined early in the straight to win by a length and a quarter.

Our Boy Stan is out of Whoops A Daisy who was a bumper winner herself and went on to win four of her seven starts over hurdles for Nicky Henderson at up to three miles, with her biggest win coming in a listed race for mares at Kempton. She is now the dam of five winners, with the pick of Our Boy Stan's siblings being useful hurdler Go Dante who won the Imperial Cup for the second year running in March. Our Boy Stan's full sister Fresh As A Daisy made a successful debut over hurdles at Uttoxeter in May. **Ben Pauling**

Conclusion: *Confirmed debut promise in the listed junior bumper at Cheltenham when successful at Kempton and has the pedigree to make an above-average novice hurdler*

Realco
b103

5 b.g. Falco (USA) – Maori Legend (Midnight Legend)
2024/25 b16.7v* b16.3s² Feb 8

Worcestershire trainer Tom Weston tends to have a handful of winners at most under Rules each season, but his business is mainly concerned with developing young horses in bumpers and points with a view to selling them on to other yards. A successful graduate from this nursery is Boombawn who was sold to join Dan Skelton for £55,000 after finishing second on his bumper debut for Weston. Boombawn made into a useful hurdler for his new connections and did better still over fences last season, showing smart form and winning the Rising Stars Novices' Chase at Wincanton.

Skelton must now be hoping for something similar from Realco, he too purchased from Weston after showing plenty in bumpers. He had two runs for his former trainer in the spring of 2024, finishing third of four on his debut at Chepstow and then winning at Uttoxeter. Skelton had to go to £80,000 to secure Realco at the Goffs UK Aintree Sale but was in no hurry to send him over hurdles and instead gave him two more runs in bumpers last season. He had no trouble making a winning start for his new connections when notably strong in the betting at Exeter in January and then ran well in the listed bumper on Newbury's 'Super Saturday' the following month. Winning favourite Sober Glory completed a hat-trick while Realco kept on to take second in the final 100 yards, finishing a length and three quarters behind the winner.

Those efforts should offer a solid platform for the good-topped Realco to switch to hurdling this season. He's by Falco who has had some talented although not entirely straightforward jumpers such as Triumph Hurdle winner Peace And Co and Paul Nicholls' smart chaser Hitman. Realco is a first winner for his dam Maori Legend, a fair chaser who won three times at around three miles, while Grand National winner Royal Athlete is further back in the family. Realco has done all his racing in bumpers in the mud and he's likely to need further than two miles over jumps. ***Dan Skelton***

Conclusion: *Showed useful form in testing conditions in bumpers and can build on that in novice hurdles for his top stable*

Ben Linfoot (Realco): *"There's no shame in getting beat in the Newbury bumper on 'Super Saturday'—just look at Buveur D'Air and Altior—and Dan Skelton's Realco enhanced his reputation in defeat behind Sober Glory in the February fog. His dam was a three-mile chase winner and that's where he could be heading, too, but not before a potentially fruitful campaign in staying novice hurdles."*

Rubber Ball   h124

5 b.g. Yorgunnabelucky (USA) – Psychocandy (Ire) (Oscar (Ire))
2024/25 b16.4g⁵ h21s³ h15.8s³ h15.8s* h16.3s* h16.5g Apr 4

The sire Yorgunnabelucky—a full brother to the top-class Shamardal—was well advertised last season by Libberty Hunter, a smart and likeable two-mile chaser who won a handicap at Cheltenham, finished second in the Game Spirit Chase at Newbury and wasn't done with when falling three out in the Queen Mother Champion Chase. Novice hurdler Rubber Ball was another to do well for the sire last season, and he could well be capable of better things over fences this term.

After finishing fifth in a bumper at Cheltenham in October on his debut under Rules, Rubber Ball was soon switched to hurdles and progressed with each run until his final outing. He made his debut over hurdles at Warwick over 21 furlongs, finishing third of the five runners, but was dropped back to around two miles for his remaining starts. He was third again next time behind another two of our *Fifty*, Vanderpoel and George's Lad, in a maiden at Huntingdon and then got off the mark in a similar event at Uttoxeter later in January. He was well backed and comfortably landed the

Rubber Ball (left) won at Newbury during a promising novice hurdle campaign

odds by 11 lengths after making most of the running. Rubber Ball looked to have more on his plate in a novice at Newbury the following month where Tutti Quanti and Kientzheim dominated the betting at 11/8 and 6/5 for Paul Nicholls and Nicky Henderson respectively in a field of five. But with soft ground putting the emphasis on stamina, Rubber Ball proved well suited by the test and won by a length after heading Tutti Quanti in the final furlong.

The runner-up went on to show useful form, but Rubber Ball's progress stalled when faced with a stiff task as a 40/1 shot in the Top Novices' Hurdle at Aintree. It wasn't just the better company that found him out as conditions weren't as soft as for his previous starts over hurdles. Even so, he looks the type to do well over fences this term, being a tall gelding who won his only start in Irish points, and he looks worth another try beyond two miles. **Neil King**

Conclusion: *Winning pointer who progressed well on soft ground over hurdles before he was set a stiff task at Aintree; appeals as the type to do well over fences*

Skuna Bay (Ire)   h107

6 b.g. Mahler – Miss Island (Ire) (Dr Massini (Ire))
2024/25 h20d³ h19.6v⁴ h19.7s² Feb 1

A trio of maiden hurdles at trips around two and a half miles failed to present enough of a stamina test for the stoutly-bred Skuna Bay, but it's encouraging that the pointing graduate managed to finish in the frame on each start, and he's expected to raise his game over longer distances.

There are no mixed messages in Skuna Bay's pedigree as he is by Mahler, sire of stayers such as Troytown winners Chris's Dream and The Big Dog, and out of a half-sister to Mister Malarky, a smart handicap chaser at his best who stayed three and a quarter miles. Skuna Bay, who was picked up relatively cheaply at £25,000 having finished placed on both starts in Irish points, duly shaped like the stayer he is bred to be when third on his debut under Rules at Carlisle in November, losing ground when outpaced approaching the second last before keeping on again up the run-in. Skuna Bay ran to just a similar level when fourth at Bangor the following month, but he took a step forward on his final start of the campaign at Wetherby where he found only the form pick too strong. He had the run of the race to an extent at Wetherby, but he still impressed with some slick jumping, and he refused to lie down when headed two out and rallied to regain second.

Given his pointing background, pedigree and physique—he's a rangy, chasing type—he has all the hallmarks of one who will come into his own over fences this season, especially when faced with a proper test of stamina. A BHA handicap mark of 115 is stiff enough strictly on what he has shown so far, but we've only just started to scratch the surface and it would be little surprise to see Skuna Bay develop into a useful novice chaser. **Donald McCain**

Conclusion: *Staying chaser in the making who should step up on his hurdling efforts when tackling longer distances over fences*

Soldier's Leap (Ire) h93

5 b.g. Soldier of Fortune (Ire) – Lindy Lou (Hernando (Fr))
2024/25 h16g h16g⁶ h16.3v h17.7s² h16.9d² h15.8d³ Feb 20

After riding winners between the flags, Tom Ellis turned his attention to training pointers with great success, becoming champion in that sphere five times since 2019 and setting a record for the most point winners in a season. Some of Ellis's pointers carried their success over to hunter chases, most notably Latenightpass who won the Aintree Foxhunters' in 2022, ridden by wife Gina Andrews. Latenightpass was entrusted to good friend and fellow Warwickshire trainer Dan Skelton to prepare for the 2024 Grand National, but for the Aintree bid itself Ellis took out a professional licence and Latenightpass was his first runner as a licenced trainer; he gave an exhibition display of jumping over the big fences but didn't last home.

Ellis had his first winner as a licenced trainer in September 2024 and ended his first full season with 11 winners. The now 12-year-old Latenightpass remained the stable's flagship horse and was twice placed over the cross-country course at Cheltenham, notably when runner-up at the Festival. A much younger stablemate who should be contributing to the stable's tally this season is Soldier's Leap. He was beaten a neck on his sole start in points for Andrews (who has taken over the stable's pointers, training as Georgina Ellis) before embarking on a hurdling campaign, with Andrews and her brother Jack sharing the rides. Soldier's Leap was beaten a long way in his first three appearances, twice starting at 250/1, but fared much better once switched to handicaps and was placed in all three of them, improving a little each time.

Despite racing keenly, Soldier's Leap sustained his effort well when runner-up on his handicap debut at Fontwell in December in a race where the first three pulled a long way clear, and he was then second again at Newcastle the following month when fitted with a tongue tie for the first time. Tongue tied again and returning from a breathing operation, Soldier's Leap was beaten a similar distance when third to Kingoftheswingerz in a novice handicap at Huntingdon on his final start where a last-flight blunder possibly cost him victory. A brother to Hombre de Guerra who won a couple of novice handicaps over fences last season, Soldier's Leap looks the type to win races over fences himself. **Tom Ellis**

Conclusion: *Chasing type who was placed in all three handicaps over hurdles and promises to open his account before long*

Some Bro (Ire) 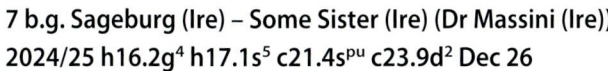 c84

7 b.g. Sageburg (Ire) – Some Sister (Ire) (Dr Massini (Ire))
2024/25 h16.2g^4 h17.1s^5 c21.4s^{pu} c23.9d^2 Dec 26

Some Bro has just poor form to his name over fences—though even that is in advance of what he achieved over hurdles—but he certainly showed enough in his two starts over the larger obstacles to suggest that there are races to be won with him at an ordinary level. He began his career in Ireland where he finished well held on his sole start there over hurdles but showed some ability in a handful of points, finishing placed on a couple of occasions. His first two runs for Mark Walford in novice hurdles at around two miles at Hexham and Carlisle were doubtless insufficient tests and he finished well held, but it was a different story when switched to fences.

Some Bro made his chasing debut in a novice handicap at Market Rasen in November and was in the process of showing much-improved form when an unfortunate incident ended his race. Having survived a bad mistake much earlier in the race, Some Bro made headway to look a big threat in second place at the third last. He took it cleanly but slithered on landing, coming to a virtual standstill which gave his jockey Jamie Hamilton little option but to pull him up. Had he kept his feet, he would likely have finished second at worst behind winner Camino Rocio.

Back at the same track for a similar event over a longer trip on Boxing Day, Some Bro was well supported following his promising chasing debut but was again undone by a late error. His jockey on this occasion, incidentally, was Dougie Costello, a Cheltenham Festival winner and a once familiar name at northern jumps tracks who plies his trade mainly on the Flat these days—his ride on Some Bro was his first over jumps for exactly three years. It could well have been a winning one but, having pulled his way to the front early on, Some Bro was headed following a bad mistake two out and was beaten a length and a quarter by Asa with the pair well clear. Some Bro wasn't seen out again last season so he remains lightly raced under Rules and should be capable of opening his account this term. **Mark Walford**

Conclusion: *Well up to winning ordinary handicaps over fences judged on the promise of his two chase starts at Market Rasen where late errors spoilt his chances*

Starzand (Ire) b106p

5 b.g. Harzand (Ire) – Phoenix Twist (Ire) (Kalanisi (Ire))
2024/25 b15.8d* Mar 21

Has the maiden bumper at the Ffos Las meeting the week after the Cheltenham Festival thrown up another future Grade 1-winning jumper? In 2023 it was won by The Jukebox Man, winner of last season's Kauto Star Novices' Chase before meeting with a setback, and last year it went to Potters Charm, he too a Grade 1 winner on Boxing Day in the Formby Novices' Hurdle at Aintree. The latest winner Starzand has some tough acts to follow, therefore, but he made an impressive winning debut and looks sure to go on to better things himself.

Starzand had recently won the second of his two Irish points by a wide margin which resulted in his topping the Tattersalls Cheltenham January Sale. With former stable jockey Richard Johnson making the successful bid of £230,000, Starzand was bought to join a growing number of horses in the string of Dave Lewis's Gwent Holdings trained by Philip Hobbs & Johnson White. Starzand faced only four rivals on his Ffos Las debut, two of whom had already shown a fair level of form in bumpers. But that pair were left trailing behind the three newcomers, with 13/8 favourite Starzand surging right away at the end. Racing freely with little pace early on, he was still going well when produced to lead under three furlongs out and, after briefly running green, came away to win by seven and a half lengths from the Sam Thomas-trained second favourite Whiskey Yankee.

Described by Johnson at the sale as 'a proper three-mile chaser' for the future, Starzand is by Derby winner Harzand who had a breakthrough season with a couple of juvenile hurdlers of note, Hello Neighbour in Ireland and Six Figures in France. Starzand's dam Phoenix Twist was only an ordinary handicapper on the Flat in Ireland, winning at Bellewstown over a mile and three quarters, and didn't show a great deal over hurdles, but she is a half-sister to Mermaids Cave, who has had a very productive time over hurdles since the beginning of last season, and to useful Irish chaser Speaker Connolly who stayed 21 furlongs. **Philip Hobbs & Johnson White**

Conclusion: *Sale-topping ex-Irish pointer who made an impressive bumper debut at Ffos Las and very much the type to do well in novice hurdles*

Strong Run   b97
6 b.m. Passing Glance – Strong Westerner (Ire) (Westerner)
2024/25 b15.8d² b16.4g³ b16s* b17g⁶ Apr 3

A sure sign of getting older is when you come across a horse's name that has been 'recycled', triggering memories of its namesake from the past. That will be the case for some with Strong Run, the Irish-bred gelding of that name being a smart chaser for Noel Meade early this century. He won the Grade 1 two-mile chase at the Punchestown Festival in 2002 and was third to Moscow Flyer in the same contest two years later. The 'new' Strong Run, a British-bred mare who is related to some very good jumpers, could well be destined to also make her mark at a high level in due course.

Strong Run showed fairly useful form in all four of her mares' bumpers, running to a similar level each time whilst looking as though the greater tests of stamina available over hurdles will see her in an even better light. After shaping very well on her debut at Uttoxeter in October behind her more experienced stablemate Dream Shadow, Strong Run was pitched into a listed contest at Cheltenham where she was just about the pick on looks in the paddock. The well-backed Irish filly Seo Linn justified the support in winning readily by five lengths, but Strong Run was one of two Fergal O'Brien mares to chase her home, keeping on in third, a neck behind stablemate Siog Geal. Strong Run had clearly shown enough by now to win an ordinary bumper, and she accomplished that task when returning from a break at Warwick in February, showing stamina and determination to get the better of longer-priced stablemate Highland Haven by a head. The first three all ran next in the Nickel Coin Mares' Bumper which Strong Run's stable had won two years previously with Dysart Enos. While Seo Linn followed up her Cheltenham win, Strong Run performed in similar fashion again, plugging on to finish a never-dangerous sixth.

The tall, useful-looking Strong Run is a sister to two winners, notably Strong Leader who also ran at the Grand National meeting, finishing second in the Liverpool Hurdle which he had won the year before. They are out of an unraced half-sister to high-class chaser Strong Flow who won the Hennessy Gold Cup as a novice for Paul Nicholls in 2003, so there's plenty of stamina in Strong Run's pedigree. **Fergal O'Brien**

Conclusion: *Showed plenty of ability in mares' bumpers but has the looks and pedigree of one who will be suited by much more of a test over hurdles*

Terrorise   h100p

4 b.g. Territories (Ire) – Timely Words (Galileo (Ire))
2024/25 h17g^{pu} :: 2025/26 h16.6g^3 h17.2d* May 28 (Sep 9 2025F)

Perhaps inspired by the exploit of Poniros the previous month who won the Triumph Hurdle at 100/1 on his debut over jumps, Terrorise made his own hurdling debut in the Anniversary 4-Y-O Hurdle at Aintree but not with anything like the same success. The rank outsider at 150/1, he proved well out of his depth before being pulled up three out. But Terrorise is a fairly useful staying handicapper on the Flat, and he showed much more promise when set far more realistic tasks on his two other starts over hurdles the following month.

After Aintree, Terrorise began the new season finishing third in a maiden at Market Rasen behind the two market leaders, Howth and All Well And Good, racing in touch before getting outpaced early in the straight. All three won their next starts, with Terrorise opening his account in a novice at Cartmel. He needed every yard of the trip but justified the strength behind him in the betting to come out on top in a three-way finish. After an awkward jump at the last, Terrorise was still only fifth and looked held early in Cartmel's long finishing straight but he rallied well in the final furlong and got up to win by a short head and a neck from Celestial Reign and Spit Spot. Now qualified for handicaps, he'll be suited by two and a half miles and remains capable of better, especially when stepped up in trip.

It's not surprising that Terrorise shapes as though in need of further over hurdles as he stays well on the Flat. That's in keeping with plenty of stamina on the dam's side of his pedigree as his unraced dam is closely related to Joseph O'Brien's Melbourne Cup winner Rekindling. After his win at Cartmel, Terrorise was returned to the Flat over the summer and proved better than ever on a first try at two miles on the level when a four-length winner at York in July. That suggests he will be well up to exploiting a BHA mark of 105 over hurdles this season. **Brian Ellison**

Conclusion: *Looks well handicapped over hurdles judged on his fairly useful form as a stayer on the Flat which also suggests he'll be suited by longer distances*

The New Lion   h161p

6 b.g. Kayf Tara – Raitera (Fr) (Astarabad (USA))
2024/25 h19.5d* h20.5d* h20.5d* h21d* Mar 12

The Irish had dominated the Turners Novices' Hurdle at the Cheltenham Festival since Willoughby Court scored for local trainer Ben Pauling in 2017, but The New Lion put an end to that streak by producing a performance good enough to win Timeform's leading novice hurdler award.

The New Lion had won his only start in bumpers and his first three outings over hurdles, most notably the Grade 1 Challow at Newbury which he won in a canter under Harry Skelton. So impressive was that display that it prompted trainer Dan Skelton to comment 'he is just a very unassuming horse at home with bundles of ability, and you have to say he's as good a novice hurdler that we've had'.

The New Lion, who was purchased by JP McManus prior to the Cheltenham Festival, faced a much sterner examination in the Turners against fellow Grade 1 winners and unbeaten hurdlers Final Demand and The Yellow Clay. Final Demand, a 12-length winner of the Nathaniel Lacy and Partners Solicitors Novice Hurdle on just his second start for Willie Mullins, was the 6/4 favourite to provide his yard with a fourth consecutive win in the race, while The Yellow Clay, winner of the Lawlor's of Naas Novice Hurdle that Envoi Allen and Bob Olinger had won en route to success in the Turners, was strong in the betting and a 5/2 chance for Gordon Elliott. The New Lion was 3/1 third choice in the market but came out on top in a race-of-the-Festival contender that saw the three principals jump the final flight in a line.

The New Lion, played latest of all, was brave and long at the last, and he also showed a fine attitude under pressure up the run-in, keeping on to edge ahead of The Yellow Clay inside the final 50 yards and score by three quarters of a length. Dan Skelton,

Harry Skelton celebrates The New Lion's victory in the Turners Novices' Hurdle

refreshingly, didn't hesitate to nominate a Champion Hurdle campaign for The New Lion who looks to have the tools to cope with a well-run two miles and can make his mark in a division blown wide open by the travails of Constitution Hill. **Dan Skelton**

Conclusion: *Timeform's leading novice hurdler following his defeat of Final Demand at the Cheltenham Festival; has the speed to drop in trip and be campaigned with the Champion Hurdle in mind*

Tom Doniphon (Fr)   h117

6 br.g. Great Pretender (Ire) – La Courtille (Fr) (Risk Seeker)
2024/25 h18.5d^3 h19.7d^2 h19d* h19s* h19.8s^2 Feb 13

A tally of 53 winners last season represented a significant improvement on the 34 registered by Philip Hobbs and Johnson White during their first full campaign with a joint-licence in 2023/24. What's more, those winners came at a strike rate of 19.3% (it had been 13.2% the previous season) and placed them fifth by that metric among trainers who had at least 250 runners over jumps in Britain last term.

Tom Doniphon added two wins to his yard's tally last season and looks likely to contribute again. A useful bumper performer, Tom Doniphon shaped better than the distance beaten would suggest when third on his hurdling debut at Exeter in October. He was ultimately left behind by the front pair, Ambion View and Ace of Spades, who pulled 13 lengths clear, but he impressed with how he went through most of the race before the lack of a recent outing told. Tom Doniphon duly built on that promise and went much closer on his next outing at Hereford where he was collared in the final strides and denied by a short head.

Those two placed efforts meant Tom Doniphon was eligible for a quick switch to handicaps, and he justified that decision with another improved display to get off the mark over hurdles at Taunton. That comprehensive five-and-a-half-length success came in a conditional jockeys' handicap which meant Tom Doniphon didn't have to carry a penalty back at Taunton when wisely turned out quickly before the BHA handicapper had a chance to reassess him. As had been the case nine days earlier, Tom Doniphon impressed with how sweetly he travelled and scored with plenty in hand.

The hat-trick bid was foiled at Sandown, but he again moved like a well-handicapped horse only for testing ground, over a slightly longer trip than he'd previously tackled, to place too much of an emphasis on stamina. He was beaten by one who proved better suited by a slog, but Tom Doniphon is expected to resume his progress this season, especially if sent chasing as his well-made physique and enthusiastic style offer encouragement he'll do well over fences. **Philip Hobbs & Johnson White**

Conclusion: *Progressed well in handicap hurdles for his resurgent stable and has the tools to take well to chasing*

Tutti Quanti (Fr)   h135

5 b.g. Chanducoq (Fr) – Terebella (Fr) (Muhtathir)
2024/25 h15.8d* h16.3s² h16.4d⁶ h15.8d* Apr 6

The blue and yellow quartered silks of owner Colm Donlon are most closely associated with the very smart hurdler Langer Dan who completed the notable feat of winning back-to-back editions of the Coral Cup at the Cheltenham Festival in 2023 and 2024. However, any hopes of a third successive win at the Festival were dashed when Langer Dan was ruled out of the Stayers' Hurdle with what was believed to be a respiratory issue but what transpired to be an underlying heart problem that necessitated his retirement. It will not be easy for Donlon to find another horse as talented as Langer Dan, who also won the 2021 Imperial Cup and finished runner-up to subsequent Cheltenham Gold Cup winner Galopin des Champs in the Martin Pipe Conditional Jockeys' Handicap Hurdle only six days later, but he has a nice prospect in Tutti Quanti.

Tutti Quanti was never likely to add to Donlon's Festival tally as he was sent off at 125/1 for the Supreme Novices' Hurdle, in which he was the sole representative from Britain, and he predictably failed to land a blow on the best of the Irish who filled the first five positions. However, he fared about as well as could have been expected and ran on past beaten horses in the straight. That was Tutti Quanti's third start of a campaign which started with a smooth success in a two-mile novice hurdle at Ffos Las before he found only fellow *Horse To Follow* Rubber Ball too strong in a similar event at Newbury. The Supreme, therefore, represented a huge rise in class for Tutti Quanti, but he was back in much calmer waters on his final start of the season at Ffos Las where he made the most of a good opportunity to win with ease. It's difficult to weight up exactly what Tutti Quanti achieved there, but the form of his reappearance win at the same venue worked out nicely as the runner-up won his three subsequent starts. The form of his runner-up effort in a maiden hurdle at Taunton on his stable debut the previous season is also worth noting as he was beaten only half a length by subsequent easy William Hill Hurdle winner Joyeuse.

Tutti Quanti has raced exclusively at around two miles for his current stable but is likely to stay two and a half miles if continuing to harness his exuberance, and as a tall sort he has the physique to make a chaser. **Paul Nicholls**

Conclusion: *Unsurprisingly came up short in the Supreme Novices' Hurdle but there was a lot to like about his other efforts last season and he's a useful prospect for novice chases*

Vanderpoel (Ire)   h125

6 b.g. Sholokhov (Ire) – Dear Songbird (Ire) (Millenary)
2024/25 h15.8s* h15.8s* h18.1d^{pu} Mar 1

Pedigree can sometimes count for a lot in horse racing and it seems the same is true in cycling. A world champion in more than one discipline of the sport and a winner of the Tour of Britain in 2019, Belgian-born Mathieu van der Poel is the son of a stage winner of the Tour de France, while on his 'dam's side', his grandfather was the popular French cyclist Raymond Poulidor who famously never won the Tour de France despite finishing second three times and third on another five occasions—his surname has even entered the French language to describe a perpetual runner-up and is sometimes applied to racehorses. His grandson's latest Tour de France began so well that van der Poel was in the yellow jersey after outsprinting eventual Tour winner Tadej Pogacar to win Stage 2, but in the final week he had to abandon the race suffering from pneumonia.

Last season it was pretty much the same story for the equine Vanderpoel who, in the 'yellow jersey' of owner Lady Dulverton, made an excellent start to his campaign only to pull up on his final outing. That last run in the Premier Novices' Hurdle at Kelso can be

Vanderpoel strode to an effortless success at Ludlow and is open to improvement

ignored as he probably overdid things in front, taking a strong hold, before soon stopping to nothing once headed two out. Vanderpoel is much better judged on his first two starts over hurdles, winning both of them. He started off in a maiden hurdle at Huntingdon in January, jumping accurately in a share of the lead and going with zest before being driven out to beat the next-time-out winners George's Lad and Rubber Ball who are also among our *Fifty*. Vanderpoel was then found a very uncompetitive novice at Ludlow the following month for his next start and he landed short odds with ease, again going with enthusiasm and making all the running to come home eight lengths clear.

Vanderpoel won the second of his two starts in Irish points before joining Ben Pauling's stable for €90,000. He's by Sholokhov, sire of the latest Stayers' Hurdle winner Bob Olinger, as well as the likes of Shishkin and Don Cossack. His unraced dam is a half-sister to a couple of winning chasers, including useful Irish mare up to two and a half miles Gentle Alice, and Vanderpoel should do well switched to fences himself. **Ben Pauling**

Conclusion: *Winning pointer whose last run shouldn't detract from the promise of his earlier wins that indicate a bright future over fences*

Walk Tall (Ire)   b92

5 b.g. Walk In The Park (Ire) – Blixt (Ire) (Yeats (Ire))
2024/25 b16.7v² Feb 21

Susan and John Waterworth enjoyed a particularly successful season with their string last term, with the highlight coming at Ascot in February when second-season chaser The Changing Man gained a belated first win over fences in the Reynoldstown Novices' Chase before First Confession landed a novice hurdle on the same card. The Changing Man, who carries the couple's black and white colours, was also runner-up in four valuable handicap chases during the season, the Rehearsal at Newcastle, the Silver Cup at Ascot, the Great Yorkshire at Doncaster and the Ultima at the Cheltenham Festival. First Confession, on the other hand, is owned jointly by the Waterworths with Kevan Leggett, a partnership which was also represented successfully last season by the useful chaser Scarface and by a pair of bumper horses who finished first and second in the same race at Exeter less than a week after that big day at Ascot.

In a tight finish where just a length or so covered the first four home, it was much the longer-priced of the pair, both trained by Joe Tizzard, who came out on top, with Claim The Throne stepping up on his two previous runs to cause a 25/1 surprise under Harry Cobden. Stablemate Walk Tall, on the other hand, was better fancied at 5/1 despite making his debut under Rules, but he showed plenty of ability against more experienced bumper horses to finish a half-length second having disputed the lead for much of the way under Brendan Powell before sticking to his task. The winner of his only start in Irish points, after which he joined the Tizzard stable for £120,000 at the Cheltenham December Sale, Walk Tall—who is by the same sire as The Changing Man, Walk In The Park—looked the best jumping prospect in the field at Exeter.

Walk Tall is related to a jumping legend in Hurricane Fly, the dual Champion Hurdle winner being a half-brother to Walk Tall's dam Blixt who was also trained by Willie Mullins. While nowhere near as talented, she had more stamina than her half-brother, winning twice over hurdles including a three-mile handicap at Clonmel. Another of Hurricane Fly's half-sisters produced the same stable's shock 2021 King George winner Tornado Flyer. **Joe Tizzard**

Conclusion: Winning pointer from the family of Hurricane Fly who showed promise for a jumping career when runner-up on his bumper debut

Wellington Arch   h131

6 b.g. Blue Bresil (Fr) – Moyliscar (Terimon)
2024/25 h16.7g² h17s* h18.6d² h16.6g* h19.9s² h20g* h20.5d³ May 3

Wellington Arch was arguably fortunate to win the valuable two-and-a-half-mile handicap hurdle at Aintree's Grand National meeting, so strongly did Kopeck de Mee storm up the run-in, but you make your own luck to some extent and the tough, consistent front runner Wellington Arch has traits that should ensure he continues to get 'lucky'.

That neck victory, with the pair four lengths clear of the third, was the undoubted highlight of a productive first campaign over hurdles which yielded three wins. Wellington Arch won two of his four starts in novice company, landing the odds at Carlisle and Market Rasen, and then produced a promising display on his handicap debut at Uttoxeter where he was beaten by only a lightly-raced rival making his first start for Dan Skelton. Wellington Arch had been ridden with a bit more restraint in the early stages at Uttoxeter but reverted to the free-wheeling style that suits him so well at Aintree. He moved his way to the front after the second flight, travelled sweetly and then impressed with how he quickened away from the pack on the run between the final two flights. He was ultimately all out to fend off Kopeck de Mee, who may well have won had he got rolling earlier, but time is likely to show that the runner-up is a smart sort.

Wellington Arch couldn't pull off the same aggressive tactics at Punchestown where he finished third, but that was still a creditable effort, especially when you consider he was taken on for the lead and made a momentum-halting error at the second last. That was also the first time he'd finished outside the first two in seven starts during a rock-solid campaign. That Wellington Arch fared so positively over hurdles bodes extremely well for his prospects as he has the look and demeanour of one who should raise his game further over fences. **Jonjo & A.J. O'Neill**

Conclusion: *Likeable and progressive sort who enjoyed a fine campaign over hurdles and can do even better when tackling fences*

Wendigo (Fr)   h136

6 br.g. Great Pretender (Ire) – Biche d'Oo (Fr) (Martaline)
2024/25 h16.2s² h21.2d* h20.5d² h19.7v* h24d⁵ Mar 14

Some big names have won Newbury's Challow Novices' Hurdle over the years and the unbeaten winner of the latest renewal, The New Lion, could well prove among the very best to have won the Grade 1 contest. But a roll call of some of the horses that have been placed in the Challow doesn't make for bad reading either, featuring the likes of Finian's Rainbow, Al Ferof, Blaklion, Politologue and last season's Kauto Star Novices' Chase winner The Jukebox Man.

The Jamie Snowden-trained mare You Wear It Well, who went on to success at the Cheltenham Festival later the same season, was runner-up in the 2022 Challow and the same stable went close again in the latest renewal with Wendigo who ran an excellent race to finish runner-up at 25/1. While no match for The New Lion, Wendigo rallied well approaching the last and stuck to his task to come home in front of the much shorter-priced pair Bill Joyce and Regent's Stroll. That effort came in between much simpler tasks for Wendigo when he landed the odds in an introductory hurdle, which he won readily at Ludlow in November, and a very ordinary novice at Wetherby in February in which he made all the running.

Wendigo made his final start of the season in the Albert Bartlett Novices' Hurdle at the Cheltenham Festival having never previously finished out of the first three; he had won his last couple of outings in bumpers the previous winter at Hexham and Catterick. Ridden more patiently as he had been at Newbury, Wendigo came fifth in the Albert Bartlett but ran every bit as well as he had done in the Challow and shaped better than the bare result in finishing around eight lengths behind winner Jasmin de Vaux. But for suffering the worst of the trouble on the inside after two out, when stumbling and almost unseating, he would surely have done better as he stayed on again after losing his place. A winning pointer in Ireland, the well-made Wendigo was one of the paddock picks at Cheltenham in terms of physique and looks a fine chasing prospect for the season ahead. He stays three miles and has done all his racing on going softer than good, including winning both his starts on heavy ground. *Jamie Snowden*

Conclusion: *Chasing type whose efforts in defeat behind The New Lion in the Challow and when meeting trouble in the Albert Bartlett make him one to follow over fences*

Wilstar (Ire) b101

5 b.g. Doctor Dino (Fr) – Star Face (Fr) (Saint des Saints (Fr))
2024/25 b16d³ b16.2s* Apr 25

The latest jumps season was a remarkable one for Olly Murphy based on a whole host of metrics. His tally of 141 winners in Britain—which was exceeded by only Dan Skelton's 179—represented a marked improvement on his previous best of 102, while a strike-rate of 24.7% was comfortably the highest of any trainer who had at least 50 runners. What's more, backing each of those runners would have generated a profit of £58.54 to £1 level stakes. Sean Bowen, deservedly crowned champion jockey having finished runner-up in the championship for the previous two seasons, was on board for 103 of Murphy's winners, including the well-bred Wilstar who has the potential to be a leading light for the partnership.

Wilstar fetched €250,000 as an unraced three-year-old in 2023—a significant sum for a store horse but not a surprising one given he's a half-brother to top-class performers

Douvan and Jonbon. Douvan won eight times at the highest level and, with a peak Timeform rating of 182p, remains the highest-rated horse trained by Willie Mullins, while Jonbon had won four Grade 1s at the time of Wilstar's purchase and has since added another six to his haul. Hopes were high, therefore, when Wilstar made his debut in a bumper at Warwick in March. He was unable to reward his supporters who sent him off the 6/5 favourite in a 14-runner field, but he shaped with plenty of encouragement in third behind Destination Dubai, a previous winner who went on to give the form a notable boost by finishing runner-up in the Grade 2 bumper at Aintree's Grand National Festival.

Wilstar confirmed that debut promise when getting off the mark in style at Perth on the penultimate day of the jumps season. Again sent off a hot favourite, Wilstar was ridden with patience but made steady headway out wide on the turn into the straight and impressed with how he quickened up down the outside to lead over a furlong out before scampering three lengths clear. The way he stamped his class on proceedings suggests that he's inherited plenty of the family ability and he'll be one to note in good-quality novice hurdles. His sire Doctor Dino, whose progeny includes multiple Grade 1-winning hurdlers State Man and Sharjah, tends to impart plenty of speed. **Olly Murphy**

Conclusion: *Will struggle to emulate his siblings Douvan and Jonbon, but he made a promising start to his career in bumpers and is an exciting prospect for a yard that is bidding to build on an exceptional campaign*

Wolf Moon h121

5 b.g. Pether's Moon (Ire) – Cutielilou (Fr) (Astarabad (USA))
2024/25 h15.8s² h15.8s* h15.8d* h16m Apr 26

Wolf Moon's novice campaign ended with a whimper when beating only one rival home on his handicap debut on the final day of the British jumps season at Sandown in April. However, the rangy Wolf Moon had previously laid some solid foundations and is expected to build on them when sent chasing.

Wolf Moon was an unconsidered 50/1 shot for a two-mile maiden hurdle at Huntingdon in January having finished unplaced on his only start in a point the previous May, but he belied those odds with a fine effort behind the odds-on favourite Palladium who had added some stardust to the card. German Derby winner Palladium, a €1.4 million purchase, looked set to clear right away on the turn for home having cruised into the lead before three out, but he was given a scare by Wolf Moon who was delivered with a challenge on the approach to the final flight and stuck to his task up the run-in without ever getting on terms.

He may have been a big price, but there didn't appear any fluke about Wolf Moon's performance, and he confirmed that positive impression when justifying favouritism in a similar event at Southwell a month later. Ridden more prominently than had been the case on his hurdling debut, Wolf Moon led approaching the second last

Wolf Moon (left) has plenty of size about him and should do well over fences

and gradually asserted up the run-in to score by a length and a quarter. The steady pace masked Wolf Moon's superiority, and it was the same story back at Huntingdon where he had to work hard to land the odds. The runner-up, winning Flat handicapper Galactic Charm, was much better suited by a test of speed around a sharp track, so it reflects well on Wolf Moon that he was good enough to get the narrow verdict following a protracted tussle. He's a half-brother to a speedy sort in Redemption Day, one of the highest-rated bumper performers of recent seasons, but Wolf Moon is a slower-maturing type than his sibling and will appreciate stiffer tests than those he was presented with in novice hurdles. **Ben Pauling**

Conclusion: *Strapping sort who showed promise in novice hurdles despite more of an emphasis being placed on speed than ideal*

Dan Barber (Wolf Moon): *"It doesn't always follow that the most physically imposing types will prove significantly better chasers than hurdlers but it's hard to avoid the belief that it will in the case of Wolf Moon, one of the best looking specimens seen in a paddock at a jumps track in 2024/25. For one, Wolf Moon didn't look cumbersome or wooden during a progressive novice hurdling campaign that saw him handle brush obstacles at Southwell for the first of his two successes, while it's worth noting his trainer has few peers when it comes to a youngster taking his form to another level for switching to the larger obstacles."*

Young Getaway (Ire)   h109

6 b.g. Getaway (Ger) – The Youngone (Ire) (Alhaarth (Ire))
2024/25 h16d³ h16.2s³ h20.3d⁴ h16.9g* h16.2g² Apr 14

Nicky Richards sustained multiple injuries, including breaking his shoulder blade and several ribs, as well as fracturing his pelvis, in a fall on the gallops at his Greystoke yard in November which resulted in his being airlifted to hospital. But happily, by February, the 68-year-old was back on a racecourse to witness his stable's most valuable success all season when Famous Bridge won the Grand National Trial at Haydock. Nells Son and The Kalooki Kid were others who won valuable handicap chases in the North over the winter, while Young Getaway appeals as one who could also have a good race in him once he goes over fences.

Young Getaway showed no more than a fair level of ability over hurdles last season, having previously contested a couple of bumpers, but he's a strong gelding and a chasing type on looks so could well leave previous form behind once switched to fences. He didn't run a bad race all season, either, making the frame in all five of his starts, and while his one try over two and a half miles at Newcastle in January was a bit below his form over shorter, he still finished fourth behind some fairly useful types and should prove at least as effective over that far.

Returned to Newcastle the following month for a maiden back over two miles, Young Getaway ran out a ready winner by five lengths from Cahier's Den after main market rival He's Bresilian all but came down two out when still looking a threat. Young Getaway's best run of the season, however, came in defeat on his final start at Hexham in April. Carrying a penalty like the winner, That One, Young Getaway ran on to be beaten three quarters of a length but may well have gone even closer with a clearer run as he had to switch soon after the last and remained short of room on the run-in. Young Getaway is a well-related gelding as his unraced dam is a sister to Iktitaf who was a high-class hurdler in Ireland for the same owner, Mrs Pat Sloan. Trained by Noel Meade, Iktitaf's Grade 1 wins included the Morgiana Hurdle, and he was still close up when falling three out in the 2007 Champion Hurdle won by Sublimity. **Nicky Richards**

Conclusion: *Showed fair form in the North in his first season over hurdles but has the look of a chaser and is with a yard that does well with such types*

Kieran Clark (Young Getaway): "Of all the potential novice chasers in the North, the one that caught my eye the most is Young Getaway. He showed plenty in just a handful of starts over hurdles—his latest run looks strong form—and is very much built to thrive over fences. Combine that with a step back up in trip and he should win his fair share this campaign starting out from a BHA mark of 112."

SECTION 2

HORSES TO FOLLOW FROM IRELAND

BACKTONORMAL (IRE)	56
DOCTOR DU MESNIL (FR)	56
ETHICAL DIAMOND (IRE)	57
FEET OF A DANCER (FR)	59
FINAL DEMAND (IRE)	59
GAMEOFINCHES	60
IL ETAIT TEMPS (FR)	61
KARL DES TOURELLES (FR)	63
KARNIQUET (FR)	63
KAWABOOMGA (FR)	64
KOPECK DE MEE (FR)	65
LOMBRON (FR)	66
LOVELY HURLING (IRE)	67
NATIVE SPEAKER (IRE)	68
PLACE DE LA NATION (FR)	69
SOLDIER IN MILAN (IRE)	70
SPREAD BOSS TED	71
STELLAR STORY (IRE)	72
THECOMPANYSERGEANT	73
VITORIO PIEL (FR)	74

Backtonormal (Ire)   h127 c142p

7 b. or br.g. Milan – Inchiquin High (Ire) (Mountain High (Ire))
2024/25 h19.3d* c17d^5 c20.7s c17d^6 c21.5d* Feb 2

Hopefully, Backtonormal will be just that—back to normal—this season. For most winners at the Dublin Racing Festival, the next stop is Cheltenham, but Gavin Cromwell reported that Backtonormal had a 'slight setback' after his win at Leopardstown in February and he had to miss the rest of the season as a result. He should be worth the wait, though, as he won the Leopardstown Handicap Chase under 5 lb claimer Conor Stone-Walsh with plenty in hand to justify strong support which made him the 11/4 favourite against 15 rivals despite his lack of experience over fences. Travelling fluently in mid-division, Backtonormal made progress two out before leading on landing over the last and asserted quickly to beat fellow novice Sequestered by three and a quarter lengths.

Backtonormal had begun his career with Mags Mullins for whom he won a bumper at Ballinrobe. He was then placed in his first three starts over hurdles, coming up against some useful types, before making a successful debut for Cromwell at the 2024 Punchestown Festival when landing the valuable Final of the Red Mills Irish EBF Auction Series. He was helped by the favourite Blizzard of Oz, who had beaten him on his previous start, making a mistake at the last but Backtonormal's strength at the finish suggested he would have won anyway.

Switched to fences on his return last autumn, Backtonormal contested a trio of beginners' chases before the turn of the year. He was beaten a long way in the second of them but otherwise shaped well with handicaps in mind without managing to reach the frame in some strong races. He duly fared much better at the Dublin Racing Festival, getting into the Leopardstown Handicap Chase near the foot of the weights. That was over 21 furlongs, but Backtonormal, by Milan out of a mare who won four times in points, should stay further still. He was himself runner-up in his sole start in points behind Wingmen who also ran at the Dublin Racing Festival, finishing second in a Grade 1 novice hurdle. Raced only on ground softer than good and effective on heavy, Backtonormal looks the type to go on improving in his second season over fences. He would also be one to note in a handicap hurdle given he's likely to be on a lower mark in that sphere. ***Gavin Cromwell***

Conclusion: *Well backed when getting off the mark over fences in the Leopardstown Handicap Chase at the Dublin Racing Festival and remains unexposed*

Doctor du Mesnil (Fr)   b112p

5 b.g. Doctor Dino (Fr) – Saint Grace (Fr) (Saint des Saints (Fr))
2024/25 b19s* Apr 20

Willie Mullins had an enviable group of bumper horses last season with the unbeaten mare Bambino Fever, who completed a double in the Grade 1 bumpers at Cheltenham and Punchestown, leading the way. Sortudo, Copacabana and Gameofinches all earned their place in the Champion Bumper field too, showing plenty of ability last term as well as promise for novice hurdles. Doctor du Mesnil, on the other hand, didn't make his debut until a month after Cheltenham but looked very much in the same bracket as his stablemates.

Doctor du Mesnil was sent off the 11/8 favourite for his bumper at Cork in April under Jody Townend who partnered Bambino Fever to her Grade 1 wins. Patiently ridden and charting a wider course than most on the soft ground, Doctor du Mesnil travelled powerfully before rapidly gaining places around the home turn. Taking over in front under two furlongs out, Doctor du Mesnil galloped on strongly to pull clear of his two closest market rivals, both of whom had shown a fair amount of ability already, with Thedeviluno 11 lengths back in second and a further 13 to Jack The Lad in third. 'He picked up in two strides and I knew I had them covered,' reported his rider. 'If he can get off the ground at all over a jump, I'd say he will be a very good horse.'

Doctor du Mesnil is by State Man's sire Doctor Dino and out of Saint Grace who won over fences in France and is a half-sister to a couple of black-type winners by Doctor Dino, including Ches Demonmirail who won a Group 1 chase in Italy in the summer. There are plenty of other good winners in France in the wider family but the familiar name in Britain will be Lord du Mesnil, the one-time smart staying chaser who won Haydock's Grand National Trial and was second in the National Hunt Chase. Doctor du Mesnil won his bumper over two miles and three furlongs and also promises to stay well over jumps. **Willie Mullins**

Conclusion: *Didn't make his bumper debut until late-April but impressed in pulling clear of rivals who had shown ability; should stay well and is an exciting prospect for novice hurdles*

Ethical Diamond (Ire) h143
5 b.g. Awtaad (Ire) – Pearl Diamond (Ger) (Areion (Ger))
2024/25 h16g h16.2s* h16.8d⁴ h16d Apr 12 (Aug 23 2025F)

In August, Willie Mullins won his third Ebor, and second in three years, with Ethical Diamond who was successful in the same colours that had been carried by Absurde two years earlier. Ethical Diamond showed further improvement at York to defy an 8 lb higher mark than when winning the Duke of Edinburgh Stakes at Royal Ascot. It was another Royal Ascot winner who chased him home in the Ebor where he quickened clear of Ascot Stakes winner Ascending in the final furlong. Ethical Diamond's smart Flat form clearly opens up opportunities at Group level, but it also suggests that he'll be well up to adding to a maiden success over hurdles when he goes back over jumps.

One thing that is for sure is that Ethical Diamond won't be going for the Melbourne Cup which Absurde ran in following his Ebor victory and is due to contest for a third time

The form Ethical Diamond showed to win the Sky Bet Ebor suggests he's on a lenient mark over hurdles

this autumn. Mullins revealed that Ethical Diamond has a screw in his leg as a result of a past injury and would therefore not pass the strict veterinary screening for Melbourne Cup runners. Absurde was seventh in his first Melbourne Cup venture, but the following spring landed a big handicap back over hurdles in the County Hurdle and that may well be just the sort of race for Ethical Diamond. He was fourth in the latest edition, a place behind Absurde in a contest won by their stablemate Kargese, and could hardly have shaped much better from what proved an impossible position. Dropped out under Patrick Mullins and still with just one behind him when going strongly two out, Ethical Diamond passed ten rivals once the pace lifted but could make no further impression from the last. He failed to confirm that promise in the Scottish Champion Hurdle but soon resumed his progress at Royal Ascot.

Ethical Diamond won a maiden at Limerick on the Flat for his original trainer Michael O'Meara and got off the mark over hurdles for Mullins when making all in a maiden at Punchestown prior to his County Hurdle bid. He has raced keenly in the past, but he's been more settled since fitted with a hood, and while his Punchestown win came on soft ground, most of his racing on the Flat has been under firmer conditions which Mullins feels suits him best. **Willie Mullins**

Conclusion: *Shaped very well in last season's County Hurdle before taking his form to a new level on the Flat over the summer*

Feet of A Dancer (Fr)   h137

6 b.m. Authorized (Ire) – Leah Claire (Ire) (Tomba)
2024/25 h17d* h22.8d³ h18d³ h23.4g³ h24d⁴ h20s³ Apr 21

Feet of A Dancer may not be the biggest but she's a most likeable and reliable mare and has the ability to win a bigger prize than those that have come her way so far. Her only win last season came in a conditions hurdle at Wexford, but she finished in the frame on all five subsequent starts, most notably when running a cracker in the Pertemps Final at the Cheltenham Festival.

That win at Wexford not only extended Feet of A Dancer's unbeaten course record to three, but it also underlined her very good record fresh, coming at the end of May 2024 after a four-month break. She again ran well following an absence when third in a listed mares' hurdle at Limerick in October and backed that up when filling the same position in a similar event at Punchestown a month later.

In December, Feet of A Dancer was stepped up to nearly three miles for the first time for the Pertemps Qualifier at Leopardstown, a race another mare from her stable, Mrs Milner, had used as a stepping stone on the way to winning the 2021 Final. Feet of A Dancer booked her place at Cheltenham by finishing third whilst also shaping well, moving up to lead early in the straight and sticking to her task after being headed at the final flight.

Given her record fresh, Feet of A Dancer was put aside until the Pertemps Final where she may have gone close to emulating Mrs Milner in different circumstances. In contrast to Leopardstown, she ended up being left with plenty to do under a patient ride at Cheltenham. Still well off the pace out wide two out, there were more than a dozen ahead of her turning into the straight, but a sustained run took her into fourth after the last in a race won by Doddiethegreat. Despite being easy to back, Feet of A Dancer then ran at least as well on her final start of the season at Fairyhouse when dropped back to two and a half miles. Stepping up to Grade 2 company in a competitive edition of the Rathbarry & Glenview Studs Hurdle, Feet of A Dancer finished a length and a half third to the smart winner Maxxum. Connections should have plenty of options with Feet of A Dancer who is effective at up to three miles and is capable of making her mark in mares' races and handicaps. **Paul Nolan**

Conclusion: *Goes well fresh but proved better than ever late last season, shaping with promise in the Pertemps Final*

Final Demand (Ire)   h160p

6 b.g. Walk In The Park (Ire) – Zuzka (Ire) (Flemensfirth (USA))
2024/25 h21s* h22.2d* h21d³ May 2

'You'd love to ride him down to a fence. It's the old cliché about what they do over hurdles being a bonus but this lad definitely falls into that category.' If Final Demand's jockey Paul Townend is right—and we couldn't agree with him more—he will prove to be some chaser if his novice hurdle campaign was indeed merely 'a bonus'. The winner of three of his four starts, two of those were Grade 1 contests which he won by 12 and 16 lengths respectively. His Rules debut set the tone for those performances as he was an impressive 15-length winner on his debut in a maiden at Limerick just after Christmas, beating a pair of next-time-out winners who went on to show useful form.

Final Demand was pitched straight into Grade 1 company in the Nathaniel Lacy & Partners Solicitors Novice Hurdle at Leopardstown and treated a field full of winners in much the same way as he'd dismissed the maidens at Limerick. A sound pace meant that most had cracked by early in the straight but Final Demand, after racing with plenty of zest in touch, was just starting to get going by that stage and stormed clear after leading on the bridle approaching the last to win by a dozen lengths from Wingmen. Final Demand's only defeat came when he was sent off the 6/4 favourite for the Turners Novices' Hurdle at Cheltenham where he lacked the same experience as the pair who beat him, The New Lion and The Yellow Clay, though the winner in particular is an equally exciting prospect. Final Demand edged into a narrow lead approaching the last but was joined at the final flight, which he failed to jump fluently, and could find no extra.

Final Demand and The Yellow Clay met again in the Alanna Homes Champion Novice Hurdle at Punchestown and while the latter, who narrowly started favourite, clearly wasn't in the same form as he had been at Cheltenham, Final Demand signed off with another most impressive win. Townend made full use of his relentless galloping this time, with Final Demand storming clear after the last where The Yellow Clay fell when held in third. A well-made son of Walk In The Park who had fetched €230,000 as an unraced three-year-old, Final Demand also won his only start in points and it's easy to see him taking top rank among the season's novice chasers. **Willie Mullins**

Conclusion: *Chasing type who confirmed himself one of the best novice hurdlers with a second wide-margin Grade 1 win at Punchestown; has the potential to go to the top over fences*

Gameofinches b109p
6 br.g. Blue Bresil (Fr) – Wild Blueberry (Ire) (Flemensfirth (USA))
2024/25 b16s* b16.4d Mar 12

Gameofinches was Paul Townend's mount in the Champion Bumper which was won by his sister Jody on the well-supported mare Bambino Fever who duly fared best of Willie Mullins' five runners in a more steadily-run renewal than is usually the case. A stronger gallop would have served Gameofinches better as he didn't settle fully and finished down the field in twelfth, but he shaped better than the result and, after just the one start beforehand, likely needed the experience more than most. After being held up, he initially made smooth headway but ran green when shaken up entering the straight and weakened late on.

But the well-made Gameofinches was just about the pick of the Champion Bumper field on looks and gives the impression that he's a better prospect than quite a few of those who finished in front of him. He had propelled himself to the head of the Champion Bumper betting the previous month when making an impressive debut at Punchestown in a race which Ballyburn had won for the same stable two years earlier. Sent off at odds-on under Patrick Mullins (who rode Copacabana at Cheltenham), Gameofinches travelled strongly in a handy position before being produced to lead over a furlong out and won hard held by four and a quarter lengths from second favourite Begorra Man who had had a run over hurdles, finishing fifth at Leopardstown behind the future Supreme winner Kopek des Bordes.

Gameofinches had two runs in points, falling at the last on his debut before easily making amends next time. He has a good jumping pedigree too, being by Constitution Hill's sire Blue Bresil and a half-brother to The Kalooki Kid who made into a useful novice chaser for Nicky Richards last season. Their dam Wild Blueberry was lightly raced but grandam Valleya won over hurdles and was a sister to the high-class Martin Pipe-trained hurdler Valiramix who looked all set to win the 2002 Champion Hurdle until sadly sustaining a fatal injury before two out. Gameofinches was one of only a few six-year-olds in the Champion Bumper field, as was the case with runner-up Fact To File two years earlier. Mullins sent Fact To File straight over fences the following season and was pondering taking the same route with Gameofinches this term after his Punchestown win. Either way, he's a fine jumping prospect. **Willie Mullins**

Conclusion: *Impressed on his bumper debut before finishing down the field at Cheltenham, but he was the pick on looks there and has a bright future*

Il Etait Temps (Fr) c172

7 gr.g. Jukebox Jury (Ire) – Une des Sources (Fr) (Dom Alco (Fr))
2024/25 c16.3d* c15.4m* Apr 26

Throughout his career the compact Il Etait Temps has rather lived in the shadows of some stablemates with larger physiques and bigger reputations, but the time has come for him to take top billing in the two-mile chase division.

Il Etait Temps largely played second fiddle to the previous season's Champion Bumper winner Facile Vega during his novice hurdle campaign, though he did manage to bag a Grade 1 when his stablemate underperformed at the Dublin Racing Festival. It was a similar story as a novice chaser. Stablemates Gaelic Warrior and Fact To File, who were both successful at the Cheltenham Festival, hogged the headlines, but Il Etait Temps managed three Grade 1 wins of his own, including a defeat of Gaelic Warrior at the Punchestown Festival.

It was easy to write off that Punchestown success as 'end-of-season form', a case of Il Etait Temps again capitalising on a more talented stablemate producing a below-par effort. However, Il Etait Temps showed he's a horse to underestimate at your peril when

Il Etait Temps proved better than ever when winning the Celebration Chase

returning from a year's absence to win the Celebration Chase at Sandown on the final day of the British jumps season. True, Il Etait Temps was fresh and up against some rivals who had endured tough campaigns, while the ground, described by Timeform as good to firm, was quicker than you tend to get for top-level chases nowadays. But Il Etait Temps, who impressed with how smoothly he travelled before quickening into the lead while still on the bridle between the final two fences, looked full value for his five-and-a-half-length success and has been credited with a top-class performance. A good time, even allowing for the quick conditions, also suggests it's worth taking a positive view of the race. Celebration Chase runner-up Jonbon had fluffed his lines in the Champion Chase but had otherwise looked the one to beat in the division. That distinction now belongs to Il Etait Temps. **Willie Mullins**

Conclusion: *Tough, likeable sort whose impressive performance in the Celebration Chase sets the standard in the two-mile division*

Karl des Tourelles (Fr)   h140

5 b.g. Choeur du Nord (Fr) – Shiva d'Hautefois (Fr) (Sheyrann)
2024/25 h16s h19.4s h24.1d^2 h20s^3 h24d h23.5d^4 May 1

Karl des Tourelles is yet to add to his 100/1 debut success in a juvenile hurdle at Gowran, but age is very much on his side and he shaped more than once last season as though he's up to winning a good handicap over hurdles. That debut win was no fluke as he went on to prove himself a useful juvenile when finishing second in a Grade 2 contest at Fairyhouse, but he found things tougher afterwards in better races at Punchestown and Auteuil.

Karl des Tourelles shaped at Fairyhouse as though longer trips would suit and, after a pipe-opener on the Flat earlier in the autumn, he contested a Pertemps Qualifier at Punchestown in November. He earned a place in the Final with an improved effort in second, beaten only half a length by Franciscan Rock. Travelling well before getting shuffled back before the third last, he took closer order again at the next and kept on from the last, proving himself effective at three miles. He had one other run before Cheltenham, at Limerick just after Christmas, when sent off favourite for a useful minor event over two and a half miles, and ran respectably in third behind outsider of the five Meet And Greet.

After that, Karl des Tourelles was kept fresh for Cheltenham and he played a bigger part in the Pertemps Final than finishing seventh would suggest as he pressed the leader entering the straight and lost places late on in a race won by Doddiethegreat. He fared a bit better in the Conway Piling Handicap Hurdle at Punchestown but shaped similarly, looking the most likely winner turning in but winding up fourth behind the Nicky Henderson-trained winner Jeriko du Reponet who got the better of stablemate Doddiethegreat in a reversal of their placings at Cheltenham. A good-topped gelding, Karl des Tourelles stays three miles but should prove as effective at a bit shorter, and he acts on heavy ground. **Philip Fenton**

Conclusion: *Couldn't quite sustain his efforts after looking dangerous at Cheltenham and Punchestown but gives the impression he can win a good handicap hurdle*

Karniquet (Fr)   h143

5 ch.g. Kapgarde (Fr) – Queenjo (Fr) (Grand Tresor (Fr))
2024/25 h16.2v* h16g^5 h16d^2 h16.4d^4 h16g^2 Apr 6

Karniquet couldn't add to his maiden success over hurdles, for all that he ran very well in graded company, but he's a rangy sort who will make a chaser and looks the type who will win more races once he goes over fences. He finished second in both his juvenile hurdles in France early in 2024 for Isabelle Pacault, at Pau and Auteuil, but went one better straight away on joining Willie Mullins. His maiden hurdle at Tramore in November wasn't much of a jumping test as half of the eight flights were omitted, but he looked a fine prospect nonetheless in a race his stable had won two years previously with Gaelic Warrior, forging clear to win by 11 lengths.

His first venture into Grade 1 company resulted in a heavy defeat a month later in a foggy Future Champions Novice Hurdle at Leopardstown but the effort could be easily excused as, taking a strong hold in front, he all but came down at the second hurdle. Karniquet fared much better back at Leopardstown in the Tattersalls Ireland Novice Hurdle at the Dublin Racing Festival where Mullins fielded six of the ten runners. Odds-on favourite Kopek des Bordes was the only one who really mattered, storming clear in the straight to win by 13 lengths, but behind him Karniquet shaped very well in second and in turn pulled clear of the rest having travelled smoothly in rear.

His task when taking the winner on again in the Supreme Novices' Hurdle at Cheltenham was therefore a thankless one, but he showed a bit more improvement in a first-time hood in finishing fourth, a couple of lengths closer to Kopek des Bordes than he had been at Leopardstown. Karniquet's sights were lowered for his final start in the Grade 2 Donohue Marquees Novice Hurdle at Fairyhouse for which he started odds-on. He possibly wasn't over his hard race at Cheltenham, though, as he was beaten by stablemate Irancy who had finished a long way behind him in the Supreme. Karniquet is a half-brother to several winners, mostly in France, but they also include Gemirande, a useful handicap chaser for Venetia Williams who won last season's December Gold Cup at Cheltenham. Karniquet was fitted with a tongue tie for both his starts in France. **Willie Mullins**

Conclusion: *No disgrace in proving no match for stablemate Kopek des Bordes and looks very much the type to progress over fences*

Kawaboomga (Fr) h142p
5 b.g. Tunis (Pol) – Boisserie (Fr) (Saint des Saints (Fr))
2024/25 h16g² h16s* Jan 25

Kawaboomga contested only two maiden hurdles during a truncated campaign, but he showed an abundance of promise against a couple of Ireland's top novices and looks set to make his own mark in graded company.

Kawaboomga had won a bumper and finished third in a maiden hurdle for Francois Nicolle in France, and he shaped promisingly when runner-up on his first start for Willie Mullins at Leopardstown over Christmas. Kawaboomga ran to a level that would have been good enough to win most maiden hurdles, but he was unlucky to bump into an exceptional prospect from his own yard in the shape of Kopek des Bordes. The task facing Kawaboomga at Leopardstown was illustrated when Kopek des Bordes went on to slam his rivals by 13 lengths in the Tattersalls Ireland Novice Hurdle at the Dublin Racing Festival before justifying short-price favouritism with a very smart performance in the Supreme Novices' Hurdle at the Cheltenham Festival.

Kawaboomga was next seen at Fairyhouse towards the end of January. That was before Kopek des Bordes had been given the opportunity to frank the form, but Kawaboomga was still well backed and sent off favourite against a couple of rivals who had also shown ability when placed in maiden hurdles at Leopardstown's Christmas Festival. Koktail Divin, running at a time when Henry de Bromhead's stable wasn't firing on all cylinders, underperformed in a distant third, but there was still a lot to like about the way Kawaboomga and William Munny pulled clear in a fast time, with Kawaboomga proving the stronger up the run-in to score cosily by a length and a half.

That display established Kawaboomga as a genuine Cheltenham Festival contender and he was prominent in the market for the Turners Novices' Hurdle until he met with a setback and was ruled out for the rest of the campaign. He may have been on the sidelines, but his reputation grew as a consequence of how well the Fairyhouse form worked out. Koktail Divin and fourth-placed Zanoosh both won next time out as, more significantly, did William Munny who stormed clear in a listed novice at Punchestown before showing much better form when runner-up to Kopek des Bordes in the Supreme. Kawaboomga may also have proved himself one of the top novices around had injury not intervened, but, as a five-year-old, he still has time on his side and has plenty of untapped potential. **Willie Mullins**

Conclusion: *Chased home Kopek des Bordes before beating another leading novice in William Munny; can quickly make his mark in graded company*

Billy Nash (Kawaboomga): *"We only got to see Kawaboomga twice last season but what we saw was hugely encouraging. He beat all bar Kopek des Bordes at Leopardstown before running out an impressive winner of a race that worked out particularly well at Fairyhouse. The setback that kept him out of the big spring festivals was reportedly not a serious one and I expect him to take high rank in the novice chase division this term. However, if he does need some extra time off the track it is well worth pointing out that he only needs one more run over hurdles to qualify for the big handicaps at Cheltenham."*

Kopeck de Mee (Fr) h142p

5 ch.g. Masterstroke (USA) – Tartinette (Fr) (Creachadoir (Ire))
2024/25 h17.9s* h20.3d h20g² Apr 4

At one stage in the spring, Kopeck de Mee headed the ante-post betting for three handicaps at the Cheltenham Festival, the County Hurdle, the Coral Cup and the Martin Pipe. That was despite being yet to run for Willie Mullins, but bookmakers were taking no chances about JP McManus's French import who had been allotted a BHA mark of 136 for the Festival's handicaps. Trained in France by Joel Boisnard, Kopeck de Mee had won a maiden on the Flat and a couple of juvenile hurdles in the Provinces before completing a hat-trick in a listed contest at Auteuil in May 2024.

Kopeck de Mee was apparently due to go straight over fences for his new connections, but a setback meant that Mullins couldn't get a run into him before the Festival. Crucially, Kopeck de Mee had had five runs over hurdles which meant that he complied with the new eligibility rules for the Festival's handicap hurdles. As a result, Kopeck de Mee became one of the most talked about runners in the run-up to Cheltenham. In the end, the Martin Pipe was his chosen race where he started the 5/2 favourite in a field of 24. But after all the hype, Kopeck de Mee trailed home, soon done with when pushed along on the home turn and then eased off.

But at Aintree three weeks later he showed that the confidence in him hadn't been misplaced. His Cheltenham performance had dampened enthusiasm a little as he was third choice in the betting at 8/1 for a competitive premier handicap, but he showed vastly more this time, also improving on his French form. Ridden more patiently than in the Martin Pipe, Kopeck de Mee was still going well jumping two out but still had seven in front of him at that stage, including the eventual winner Wellington Arch who managed to lead throughout—but only just. Going second after the last, Kopeck de Mee reduced the winner's advantage all the way to the line and lost out by only by a neck, and he would probably have been in front within another 20 yards or so. The lengthy Kopeck de Mee is open to further improvement over hurdles, but, still only five, he'll presumably make the switch to fences now, a season later than planned. **Willie Mullins**

Conclusion: *Failed to live up to the hype on his stable debut at Cheltenham before producing a much better showing at Aintree which marked him out as one to follow*

Lombron (Fr) c146
6 br.g. Turgeon (USA) – Omememo Has (Fr) (Gentlewave (Ire))
2024/25 c20.1d⁴ c20v² c20d* c28.7m² Apr 26

Willie Mullins threw everything into his bid to retain his title as champion trainer in Britain in another battle which went down to the final day of the season at Sandown. That included fielding no fewer than ten runners in the day's big handicap, the bet365 Gold Cup, in which title rival Dan Skelton was represented by just the one runner, Hoe Joly Smoke, running from 12 lb out of the handicap. As it happened, the title had effectively been decided in the previous race where Mullins' Il Etait Temps beat odds-on favourite Jonbon in the Celebration Chase. While Mullins was out of luck in the Gold Cup, which went to the Olly Murphy-trained Resplendent Grey, he did have the next four home. They were headed by the youngest of the stable's ten, six-year-old Lombron, carrying just 10-2 and the mount of Rachael Blackmore. That was significant because it turned out to be the jockey's final ride in Britain; Blackmore announced her retirement just over a fortnight later.

Lombron could easily have been yet another noteworthy success on British soil in Blackmore's ground-breaking career. Recovering from his rider briefly losing an iron

Lombron (left) ran a cracker when runner-up in the Bet365 Gold Cup and is unexposed as a staying chaser

after a mistake five out, Lombron looked to be cantering all over his rivals when leading between the final two fences and still wasn't stopping after the last but was collared close home to be beaten a length. Even so, it was a career-best from Lombron who was something of a revelation at Sandown and will make plenty of appeal in more staying handicap chases this season.

Lombron's only success over hurdles came in a maiden at Thurles on his Irish debut after one run in France, while his chasing experience prior to Sandown amounted to just three runs in beginners' chases over fully a mile shorter than the bet365 Gold Cup. He showed plenty of ability though, finishing fourth to stablemate Lecky Watson, the future Brown Advisory winner, at Navan and then second at Gowran before making all to land the odds at Clonmel in March where he looked the type to hold his own in good handicaps. A tall gelding, Lombron's Sandown run shows he handles good to firm ground as well as heavy. **Willie Mullins**

Conclusion: *Went close in the bet365 Gold Cup on just his fourth start over fences and retains an unexposed profile in staying handicaps*

Lovely Hurling (Ire)   h142p
6 b.g. Walk In The Park (Ire) – There Is No Point (Ire) (Galileo (Ire))
2024/25 b20d* h18.5d* h20.6d² May 2

Lovely Hurling surely won't be the last horse to have a view of Final Demand disappearing into the distance after the last but there's a good chance that he'll be dealing out the same treatment to others on a few occasions this season. The two sons of Walk In The Park were both having just their fourth starts when they met in the Alanna Homes Champion Novice Hurdle at the Punchestown Festival. But while Final Demand was already a Grade 1 winner and coming off a third-place finish in the Turners Novices' Hurdle at Cheltenham, Lovely Hurling faced a big step up from winning a maiden hurdle at Naas on his previous start.

In the circumstances, Lovely Hurling shaped very well, certainly much better than being beaten 16 lengths by the winner might suggest. His jumping warmed up as the race wore on and he made a striking move from the rear to chase the eventual winner from three out until the home turn. He reduced the deficit to a few lengths early in the straight but his exertions began to tell and he tired going to the last as Final Demand stamped his authority on the race in the manner of one destined for big things over fences.

Lovely Hurling is also a good prospect, though, having been lightly campaigned to date. He was sent off at 80/1 when seventh on his debut in a maiden hurdle at Fairyhouse in March 2024, again shaping better than the distance beaten suggests given he hadn't been asked for his effort when making a bad mistake two out. Much more was evidently expected from Lovely Hurling in a bumper at Wexford on his next start a couple of months later, and he confirmed debut promise with a smooth win at odds of 6/5. It was eight months before Lovely Hurling reappeared back over hurdles for his Naas win in February which was gained easily by four lengths from the other joint favourite Autoportrait. A brother to Cadatharla, winner of the Killarney National in May for the same connections, Lovely Hurling is described by trainer Colm Murphy as a chaser in the making with plenty of size and scope. **Colm Murphy**

Conclusion: *Lightly-raced type who shaped very well when chasing home Final Demand in a Grade 1 novice hurdle at Punchestown and is set to improve further*

Native Speaker (Ire) c134

7 b.g. Court Cave (Ire) – Odonimee (Ire) (Idris (Ire))
2024/25 h24.5g³ h25g* c25.8g³ c20g* c21d³ :: 2025/26 c20.2g c22.5d Aug 1

Still lightly raced over fences, Native Speaker looks the type to win a good handicap in his second season as a chaser. He soon showed improved form for going over the larger obstacles and was much quicker to open his account over fences than he had been over hurdles. He came up against some useful types over hurdles and was placed several times before being found a winning opportunity in a maiden at Kilbeggan early last season on his seventh start over jumps.

While Native Speaker's initial try over fences at Sligo proved disappointing, he soon left that behind in a beginners' chase at Fairyhouse in November. Gordon Elliott's Will Do, with superior hurdles form, was sent off favourite but he couldn't catch Native Speaker who jumped fluently in the lead and kept on well to win by just under five lengths.

Back at Fairyhouse the following month, Native Speaker only just failed to follow up in a novice, rallying after he was headed at the last but coming off worst in a three-way finish behind two more useful novices in Judicieuse Allen and Kanturk Kalanisi.

It was the Punchestown Festival before Native Speaker was seen out again, meaning he was returning from five months off when contesting a typically competitive renewal of the listed novice handicap chase. His absence seemed to tell as he travelled better than most before dropping away from the home turn. He was still close up three out despite having hit the previous fence but was beaten a long way in the end, finishing ninth of the 13 who completed. Native Speaker then had another break until the Galway Festival but ran much closer to his best and shaped as though ahead of his mark, something he'll hopefully prove in the coming months. In another large field, Native Speaker was closing when hitting two out and challenged on the home turn, but he could find no more inside the final furlong and was beaten around five lengths in seventh. Native Speaker, who races prominently, won his maiden hurdle at just over three miles but has largely raced at shorter trips over fences so may be worth trying back over further at some stage. He's also yet to encounter testing ground over fences but had form on heavy going over hurdles. **Henry de Bromhead**

Conclusion: *Soon left hurdles form behind over fences and gave the impression he remains ahead of his mark at Galway over the summer*

Place de La Nation (Fr)   h137
4 b.f. Masked Marvel – Liberalis (Fr) (Muhtathir)
2024/25 h17.9s³ h16s² h16.8d⁵ Mar 14

Poniros wasn't the only rank outsider among Willie Mullins' 11 runners in the Triumph Hurdle to excel. A useful handicapper on the Flat for Ralph Beckett, Poniros produced a remarkable performance to win the Triumph on his first start over hurdles, while one of the best efforts from a stablemate came from Place de La Nation, she too sent off at 100/1, who was only four lengths away in fifth. Danny Gilligan's mount showed much-improved form and looked very much at home in top juvenile company for the first time.

Place de La Nation did have some hurdling experience already, though it only amounted to a couple of starts in which she had shown no better than fair form. Her debut had come the previous September for Yannick Fouin at Auteuil where she finished third in a newcomers' race for three-year-old fillies. When she made her debut for Mullins five months later at Fairyhouse, she did so against older mares in a maiden hurdle and shaped well in second behind odds-on stablemate Karoline Banbou, although flattered to be beaten just over two lengths. Karoline Banbou herself went on to run well at Cheltenham, finishing fourth in the Dawn Run Mares' Novices' Hurdle.

Unlike Poniros, the good-topped Place de La Nation, a daughter of St Leger winner Masked Marvel, is very much bred for jumping. Mullins won a maiden hurdle at Tramore with her full brother Quais de Paris who looked destined for better things but has only run once since. On the other hand, Mullins and Place de La Nation's owners Gigginstown House Stud are enjoying plenty of success with her half-brother Quai de Bourbon. The winner of three of his four starts over hurdles once joining Mullins, and third in the Martin Pipe on the other occasion, he made into a smart chaser last season despite failing to complete at Cheltenham and Aintree. Sent off favourite for the Irish Grand National, he ran a fine race to finish third to Haiti Couleurs. That suggests Place de La Nation will be well served by longer trips herself in due course, though with her novice status over hurdles preserved for another season it would be little surprise were she to head back to Cheltenham as a leading candidate for the Dawn Run. **Willie Mullins**

Conclusion: *Excelled herself at long odds when fifth in the Triumph Hurdle and can put that experience to good use against novices*

Soldier In Milan (Ire)   b107
6 b.g. Soldier of Fortune (Ire) – Time In Milan (Ire) (Milan)
2024/25 b18.8d* May 2

It will be interesting to see whose colours Soldier In Milan carries when he reappears this season. He made his winning debut under Rules in a bumper at the Punchestown Festival for owner Paul Byrne, but if following the likes of Corbetts Cross, Feronily, The Shunter and Meetingofthewaters who were other good jumpers to show early promise in his light blue silks, it wouldn't be a surprise to see Soldier In Milan join those horses in the ownership of JP McManus sooner or later. The 2022 Grand National winner Noble Yeats was another to begin his career for Byrne who therefore has a well-founded reputation as a source of future jumping talent.

Soldier In Milan was bought for €68,000 as an unraced three-year-old before winning his only start in points by a wide margin—one of our *Fifty* Chasingouttheblues was behind him in third, incidentally. That was in the spring of 2024, and it was over a year later when Soldier In Milan made his bumper debut for Emmet Mullins who completed a treble on the day at Punchestown. Most of the big field of maidens had some bumper experience already, including the Willie Mullins-trained King Rasko Grey who was sent off the 2/1 favourite ahead of Solder In Milan who was strongly supported at 5/2. They duly finished first and second, but the favourite proved no match for the impressive winner. Travelling well behind the pace, Soldier In Milan led approaching the final furlong and kept on well to beat King Rasko Grey, who took second close home, by just under five lengths.

Soldier In Milan is by Soldier of Fortune whose jumpers are headed by the Martin Pipe and Galway Plate winner Early Doors for McManus and Joseph O'Brien. Soldier In Milan is a half-brother to a couple of winners, including Time To Rocco, a fairly useful winner over hurdles and fences in Ireland at up to two and a half miles. Their unraced dam Time In Milan is a half-sister to Oscar Time who won the Paddy Power Chase and was second in the Irish Grand National. He also built up a fine record at Aintree later in his career, finishing runner-up in the 2011 Grand National and fourth in the same race two years later, and then winning the Becher Chase as a 13-year-old. **Emmet Mullins**

Conclusion: *Winning pointer who impressed when making a successful debut in a bumper at the Punchestown Festival and has a bright future over jumps*

 Spread Boss Ted h139+
8 b.g. Yorgunnabelucky (USA) – She's The Lady (Unfuwain (USA))
2024/25 h20s⁶ Apr 21

Willie Mullins hasn't dominated the Stayers' Hurdle like some races at the Cheltenham Festival—Nichols Canyon and Penhill provided his only two wins—but he could have a strong hand this season as Ballyburn and Jasmin de Vaux fill the two spots behind Gordon Elliott's Teahupoo in the ante-post betting.

Another of Mullins' horses who isn't even quoted for the Stayers' Hurdle but could be an interesting addition to the division is the lightly-raced Spread Boss Ted. He's seemingly a fragile sort as he's had a couple of lengthy absences, but he showed enough when sixth on his belated reappearance in the Grade 2 Rathbarry & Glenview Studs Hurdle at Fairyhouse in April to suggest he retains all his ability and can do better granted a clear run at things.

Spread Boss Ted was beaten nearly 12 lengths in that two-and-a-half-mile contest, but he shaped much better than the result would suggest as he made smooth headway on the home turn and looked a threat on the approach to the second last only to fade in the style of one lacking fitness on his first start for 13 months. A lack of stamina surely wasn't to blame given his best effort the previous season had been when fourth in the Albert Bartlett Novices' Hurdle at the Cheltenham Festival. The Albert Bartlett was Spread Boss Ted's first attempt at three miles and he saw the trip out well, coming from much further back than the first three who had raced prominently throughout. He remains unexposed as a stayer and would be worth his place in graded hurdles in what is often a weak division, though it would be understandable if connections opt to go chasing given he's already an eight-year-old. Either way, there are races to be won with the talented Spread Boss Ted. **Willie Mullins**

Conclusion: *Shaped much better than the result would suggest on his only start last season and there's still time for him to deliver on the promise of his Albert Bartlett effort from the previous campaign*

Stellar Story (left) had to dig deep to make a winning start over fences

Stellar Story (Ire)   c152
8 b.g. Shantou (USA) – Bally Bolshoi (Ire) (Bob Back (USA))
2024/25 h23.9d⁴ c24.2s* c24.5d⁴ c23.8v² c24.5d² c25g³ Apr 29

Stellar Story, the 2024 Albert Bartlett Novices' Hurdle winner, looks unlikely to capture a Grade 1 over fences, but he still showed smart form during his novice chase campaign while leaving the impression that even stiffer tests of stamina could bring about a bigger effort. He, therefore, strikes as a likely candidate for the most valuable staying handicaps, including races such as the Irish Grand National or Grand National.

He started his season in the Florida Pearl Novice Chase at Punchestown, a Grade 2 in which all three runners were trained by Gordon Elliott and owned by Gigginstown House Stud. In a race which developed into a dash in the straight, Stellar Story was looking vulnerable at the final fence but a mistake from Search For Glory handed him the initiative and he scrambled home from his rallying rival to score by a diminishing short head. Stellar Story was expected to build on that in the Grade 1 Long Distance Novice Chase at Leopardstown's Christmas Festival but a couple of bad errors, notably one at the tenth, harmed his chance and he ultimately trailed in last of four. However, his jumping was largely more assured in the Ten Up Novice Chase at Navan six weeks later and that enabled him to get back on the up. Again, a steady pace meant the race didn't play to his strengths, but he kept on powerfully in the closing stages to get to within a neck of odds-on stablemate Better Days Ahead—who was in receipt of 5 lb—and he may well have won had he got rolling earlier.

That earned Stellar Story a return to Grade 1 company in the Brown Advisory Novices' Chase at the Cheltenham Festival and he fared much better than he had at Leopardstown, finishing runner-up despite the modest pace placing less emphasis on stamina than expected. Stellar Story was beaten four lengths by Lecky Watson but surely would have finished closer had the race been anything like a true test at the trip. He failed to repeat that form on his final start of the season in the Champion Novice Chase at Punchestown, where he finished a distant third after making a mistake three out when still in the mix, but he remains with the potential to do better over longer distances. **Gordon Elliott**

Conclusion: *Strong stayer who has already shown smart form over fences but could do even better over marathon trips in major handicaps*

Thecompanysergeant   h135 c145
8 b.g. Kayf Tara – Shuil Gealach (Ire) (Flemensfirth (USA))
2024/25 c20.2d² c17.3d² c18.2g* c16.7s³ c24d⁶ c20g⁴ h20s³ c20.6d² ::
2025/26 h20.5d⁵ c22.5d Jul 30

Perceval Legallois more than justified his inclusion in last year's edition of *Horses To Follow* despite disappointing in the Galway Plate, and we're hoping it's going to be a similar story with another versatile sort from Gavin Cromwell's stable in Thecompanysergeant.

Perceval Legallois was only eighth when sent off favourite for the Galway Plate, and he also came up short in the Kerry National and Troytown, but he delivered in style in the prestigious Paddy Power Chase at Leopardstown over Christmas before also winning a competitive handicap hurdle at the Dublin Racing Festival. Thecompanysergeant, who like Perceval Legallois spoilt his chance at Galway by failing to jump fluently, also appeals as one who can mix hurdling and chasing to good effect. He showed useful form during his time with Denis Hogan but looks capable of doing even better for Cromwell, who enjoyed his best campaign yet last season and finished behind only Willie Mullins and Gordon Elliott in the Irish trainers' championship.

Thecompanysergeant certainly made an encouraging start for the yard when third in a handicap hurdle at Navan in January. He was then well backed for the Trustatrader Plate Handicap Chase at the Cheltenham Festival and produced a performance that probably would have rewarded the support in a typical renewal. However, Thecompanysergeant was unlucky to bump into Jagwar, one of the most progressive horses in training, and had to settle for second. That form was boosted when the third home, Masaccio, went on to land a valuable novice handicap chase at Ayr's Scottish Grand National meeting, and when the fifth, Jordans, finished runner-up in the Grade 1 Mildmay Novices' Chase at Aintree. Thecompanysergeant failed to repeat that strong form when fifth in a competitive handicap hurdle at the Punchestown Festival and then ninth in the Galway Plate, but it's still early days for him with his current stable. **Gavin Cromwell**

Conclusion: *Ran a cracker when runner-up to the progressive Jagwar at the Cheltenham Festival and looks capable of bagging a valuable handicap for his excellent yard, either over hurdles or fences*

Vitorio Piel (Fr) b105p
5 b.g. Spanish Moon (USA) – Blue Arrow (Fr) (Blue Bresil (Fr))
2024/25 b16d* May 3

While Willie Mullins had 15 winners at the latest Punchestown Festival, nine of them in Grade 1 contests, he wasn't the only Mullins who had a good week. Nephew Emmet did well from a much smaller Punchestown team of ten, four of whom were successful. They included Its On The Line who achieved the notable feat of winning the Champion Hunters Chase for the third year running. But there were also very promising bumper wins for the newcomers Soldier In Milan and Vitorio Piel, both ridden by John Gleeson.

Vitorio Piel's bumper was restricted to unraced horses—unlike Soldier In Milan he didn't have any pointing experience—and with his stablemate having won the day before, he was likewise strongly supported to start the 7/4 favourite in a field of 20. He never saw any of those rivals, however, as he made all for a ready success after quickening clear early in the straight. The Martin Brassil-trained pair It's Only A Game and Ladbroke Grove chased him home, but it was six lengths back to the runner-up and another 12 to the third. Mullins reported afterwards that Vitorio Piel, whom he also owns, 'had been showing plenty at home', adding 'I'd say he's probably more of a top-of-the-ground horse than yesterday's guy but he's an exciting horse too.'

He could therefore prove well bought at €45,000 as an unraced three-year-old. His French-based sire Spanish Moon has had plenty of useful or better jumpers in Britain or Ireland with top-class chaser El Fabiolo much the best of them, though his jumping has been letting him down lately, including at Punchestown. The obvious selling point on Vitorio Piel's page in the sales catalogue was that his unraced dam is a half-sister to Kemboy who did so well for Willie Mullins. A multiple Grade 1 winner, Kemboy was no stranger to success at Punchestown himself, winning the Festival's novice handicap chase and, three years later, landing a memorable Punchestown Gold Cup from stablemate Al Boum Photo after which winning jockey Ruby Walsh announced his retirement from the saddle. **Emmet Mullins**

Conclusion: *Related to top-class chaser Kemboy and looked a good prospect when making a winning debut in a bumper at the Punchestown Festival*

LOOKING AHEAD

SECTION 3

PATRICK MULLINS' HORSES TO FOLLOW	**76**
DARYL JACOB'S HORSES TO FOLLOW	**78**
TALKING TO THE TRAINERS	**80**
Harry Derham	80
Harry Fry	80
Nicky Henderson	81
Philip Hobbs & Johnson White	82
Paul Nicholls	83
Jonjo & AJ O'Neill	84
Ben Pauling	84
David Pipe	84
Dan Skelton	85
Jamie Snowden	86
RISING STARS	**87**
Dylan Johnston	87
Callum Pritchard	88
Conor Stone-Walsh	89
Ewan Whillans	90
STABLE SWITCHERS	**92**
ANTE-POST BETTING	**97**
King George VI Chase	97
Champion Hurdle	98
Queen Mother Champion Chase	99
Stayers' Hurdle	100
Cheltenham Gold Cup	101
Grand National	102

Patrick Mullins' Horses To Follow

Patrick Mullins, leading amateur rider and assistant trainer at Closutton, picks out five bumper horses trained by Willie Mullins worth following.

Patrick Mullins celebrates with his father, Willie, after winning the Grand National on Nick Rockett

Arcadian Emperor
4 b.g. Kamsin (Ger) – Allegro Lady (Ger) (Santiago (Ger))

We'll start with the four-year-old Arcadian Emperor who is a fine, big, beautiful horse. He's by Kamsin and won his point-to-point at Lisronagh for Sam Curling.

Mighty Park
4 b.g. Walk In The Park (Ire) – Knotted Midge (Ire) (Presenting)

We've had a lot of success with Walk In The Park progeny over the years thanks to the likes of Douvan, Min, Nick Rockett and Facile Vega. Mighty Park is a tall and athletic type and looks one to follow in bumpers this campaign. He was second in his point-to-point at Quakerstown for Donnchadh Doyle.

Love Sign d'Aunou
4 b.g. Goliath du Berlais (Fr) – Ossun (Fr) (Anabaa (USA))

We landed the Goffs Defender Bumper at Punchestown with a filly called Wonderful Everyday and she's by the stallion Goliath du Berlais. So is the gelding Love Sign d'Aunou who won his point at Loughanmore for Gerard Quinn in April and is one to follow.

Green Hint   b101
4 gr.g. Crystal Ocean – Hint of Grey (Ire) (Mastercraftsman (Ire))

Talking of that Goffs Defender Bumper form, the second from that race, Green Hint, is now with us after being trained by Stuart Crawford last season. Running in the familiar 'Double Green' colours, he had won his point-to-point at Daramona House prior to his Punchestown run. He's by Crystal Ocean and is a smaller, sharper type, reminiscent of Jasmin de Vaux who won the Champion Bumper (and the Albert Bartlett last season) for the same connections.

Heldam
4 ch.g. Doctor Dino (Fr) – Catmoves (Fr) (Medicean)

Finally, we're very familiar with Doctor Dino progeny thanks to the likes of State Man, Sharjah, Dinoblue and Jade De Grugy, and we have high hopes for his Heldam. He would be one of the very few Doctor Dinos to have won a point thanks to his victory on the Punchestown P-To-P Course in February. He's not dissimilar to State Man in physique and is very exciting.

Green Hint (green silks) showed promise when chasing home Wonderful Everyday and has joined Willie Mullins

Daryl Jacob's Horses To Follow

Daryl Jacob, assistant racing manager for owners Simon Munir and Isaac Souede, picks out five horses to look out for in the 'double green' silks.

Daryl Jacob remains a key part of the Munir and Souede operation

Kibris — f89
3 b.g. Lope de Vega (Ire) – Dark Rose Angel (Ire) (Dark Angel (Ire))

He was a good horse on the Flat for Joseph O'Brien, especially on debut when he won a 27-runner Curragh maiden. He didn't really kick on from that on the level but he's been gelded and could be one to watch in juvenile hurdles this year. He's been schooling well at Joseph's and hurdles look to have sharpened him up a bit. He should be out early in the season. *Joseph O'Brien*

Krak — h126
5 ch.g. Muhtathir – Buttercup (Fr) (Limnos (Jpn))

Krak has moved from Stuart Crawford to Nigel and Willy Twiston-Davies and he's another who has done really well over the summer. He's a five-year-old turning six and he was a nice enough hurdler, although he didn't quite see out his races on occasion. He won at Cork when last seen, though, and he's going to be a hugely exciting novice chaser this year. *Nigel & Willy Twiston-Davies*

Le Frimeur
4 b.g. Gemix (Fr) – Ty Perrine (Fr) (Assessor (Ire))

He was with Pat Doyle last year and has gone to Harry Derham and is one to follow. He's a four-year-old, was really impressive on debut in a point, and he's a fine, big, strong horse who has strengthened up really well this summer. He's an exciting horse to have for the year ahead. *Harry Derham*

Quantum Quest   h114
5 b.g. Idaho (Ire) – Blackwater Mist (Ire) (Scorpion (Ire))

This horse took a little bit of time to get the hang of things over hurdles last year but he did well for his summer holiday and looked good when winning a maiden hurdle at Kilbeggan in August. He'll be going chasing now and he we expect improvement in that sphere. He could be one for a good handicap chase and is potentially well handicapped. *Henry de Bromhead*

Raffles Dolce Vita   h122
4 b.g. Kapgarde (Fr) – Raffles Sun (Fr) (Poliglote)

He could be a bit like Intense Raffles having gone from a French yard to Thomas Gibney, and we think he's quite exciting. A son of Kapgarde, he beat Mambonumberfive, Ben Pauling's Adonis winner, at Auteuil and his French form looks pretty good. *Thomas Gibney*

Daryl Jacob pictured winning aboard Intense Raffles

TALKING TO THE TRAINERS

We asked a number of leading National Hunt trainers to pick out a chaser, hurdler and novice to follow for the coming season. Here's what they said…

Harry Derham

Wins-Runs in Britain in 2024/25	**57-274**
Highest-rated horse in training	**Brentford Hope** Timeform Rating c139

Chaser: Norn Iron (h116): "He was a consistent performer over hurdles, a fine big horse who's finally filled into his frame. A fantastic jumper and likely to improve for fences being by Solider of Fortune."

Hurdler: Filibustering (h117): "A smart juvenile last season and I feel like the best is still very much in front of him. Hopefully he can make up into a top-level two-mile handicap hurdler."

Novice: Mossy Fen Road (b104): "Did well as a bumper horse but has schooled especially well and looks to be well above average to go novice hurdling."

Harry Fry

Wins-Runs in Britain in 2024/25	**15-122**
Highest-rated horse in training	**Boothill** Timeform Rating c157

Chaser: Gidleigh Park (c155p): "Showed his versatility last season by winning a Grade 2 novice over two miles at Windsor on soft ground, before finishing a fine second in the two-and-a-half-mile Grade 1 novice at Aintree in the spring. The Haldon Gold Cup could be an ideal starting point in what we hope will be an exciting second season over fences."

Hurdler: Altobelli (h143): "Benefited from a step up in trip to win two competitive handicap hurdles at Ascot, a course that seems to bring out the best in him. For that reason, we are aiming him at the Ascot Hurdle, which could be followed by a step back up to three miles for the Grade 1 Long Walk."

Novice: Idaho Sun (b112): "He took an unbeaten record into the Champion Bumper last season, where he finished a staying on sixth having lost his position coming down the hill when he got unbalanced. Hurdles particularly well and we have high hopes for him as a novice hurdler over two to two and a half miles on soft ground."

Altobelli (left) has developed a good record at Ascot

Nicky Henderson

Wins-Runs in Britain in 2024/25   **76-396**

Highest-rated horse in training   **Jonbon** Timeform Rating c171

Chaser: Jingko Blue (c152+): "He had three runs over fences last season, winning two, including a Grade 2 novice at Windsor. Unfortunately, he then unseated at Ascot and subsequently underwent a back operation, but he's come back looking an absolute picture and is now ready to get rolling again. The plan this season will be to target all the big three-mile handicaps, where he should have plenty of opportunities to show his class."

Hurdler: East India Express (h134): "He did nothing wrong last season, running some excellent races—most notably winning at Ascot, Kempton, and Cheltenham. On pedigree, he could well appreciate a step up in trip, though we'll start him off over two and a half miles, the distance of his most recent success. He also holds the option of novice chasing, depending on how he schools over fences this autumn."

Novice: Lucky Place (h149) and **Laughing John (h95):** "**Lucky Place** won two Grade 2s over hurdles last season and now looks every inch a top-class novice chaser. He schooled impressively over fences last year and would likely have made his chasing debut then, had he not gone and won the Coral Hurdle at Ascot instead. This season, he'll start out over two and a half miles, and all being well, he has the profile of a horse

Lucky Place is considered an exciting chasing prospect by connections

who could develop into a graded novice chaser. **Laughing John** is a winner in all but name, having unseated when running very well at Chepstow. Now on a mark of 106, he looks nicely handicapped and should prove competitive in novice handicap hurdles throughout the season. With a bit of luck, he'll be able to get his head in front and hopefully rack up plenty of wins along the way!"

Philip Hobbs & Johnson White

Wins-Runs in Britain in 2024/25	**53-274**
Highest-rated horse in training	**Lowry's Bar** Timeform Rating c149

Chaser: Imperial Saint (c143): "He's a progressive, young horse that won three races at Aintree last season and I'm hoping there might be further improvement."

Hurdler: Starzand (b106p): "He won very well at Ffos Las. He's a big, strong horse that should stay well so hopefully he has good prospects over hurdles."

Novice: Sober Glory (b107): "He's similar to Starzand but the difference is Sober Glory has better, proven form already. He was entered at Cheltenham and Aintree but with the ground being on the quicker side we thought we would finish on that good note at Newbury as he's not a horse that would want quicker ground. We are likely to start him and Starzand over two and a half miles and they will probably end up over a longer trip by the end of the season."

Paul Nicholls

Wins-Runs in Britain in 2024/25	**99-550**
Highest-rated horse in training	**Pic d'Orhy** Timeform Rating c163

Chaser: Kalif du Berlais (c155p): "He's only a five-year-old and already has a BHA rating of 156. He won a Grade 1 at Aintree in the spring and, although that wasn't the hottest, he was particularly progressive with his jumping and his ability. He should improve again and will probably start off in the Haldon Gold Cup."

Hurdler: Jubilee Alpha (h132): "She won at listed level last season and will stay over hurdles. She won over two and a half miles at Cheltenham but has the speed for two, and there are a whole heap of nice races for her to run in. I wouldn't be afraid at some stage to look at a graded race where she gets 7 lb off the geldings."

Jubilee Alpha (centre) won three times during a successful novice hurdle campaign

Novice: Blueking d'Oroux (h151): "I think he could be a really smart novice if he takes to fences. We might start off at Chepstow in the novice that we use as a bit of a prep for the Rising Stars at Wincanton."

Jonjo & AJ O'Neill

Wins-Runs in Britain in 2024/25	**72-565**
Highest-rated horse in training	**Springwell Bay** Timeform Rating c153

Chaser: Monbeg Genius (c143): "Seemed to regain some of his old form in a hot Bet365 Gold Cup and something like the Becher Chase would be a good plan for him early-season."

Hurdler: Mister Meggit (h135p): "Very lightly-raced individual who ran a blinder at Aintree in the Grade 1 novice. That was very good and we have the option of hurdles or chases with him at the moment."

Novice: Bill Joyce (h134) and **Mossy Fen Coolio (unraced):** "**Bill Joyce** will love the soft ground and he is a nice chaser in the making. **Mossy Fen Coolio** won his Irish point nicely last season. He will be a staying type and we are looking forward to getting going with him."

Ben Pauling

Wins-Runs in Britain in 2024/25	**66-401**
Highest-rated horse in training	**Handstands** Timeform Rating c154

Chaser: Pic Roc (c134): "A horse we expected more from last season. He should be very competitive in some decent handicaps this season."

Hurdler: Lanesborough (h114p): "A lightly-raced individual who has a great temperament with the ability to climb the ranks."

Novice: Vanderpoel (h125): "He will go novice chasing this season and has the potential to make into a proper two-and-a-half mile novice chaser."

David Pipe

Wins-Runs in Britain in 2024/25	**50-354**
Highest-rated horse in training	**King Turgeon** Timeform Rating c140?

Chaser: Phantomofthepoints (h130): "He's going chasing this season. He has summered well and had a wind operation. He was built to be a better chaser."

Windbeneathmywings produced a sparkling performance at Ascot where he proved in a league of his own

Hurdler: Jurancon (h128p): "You cannot really knock his form so far and he's still open to improvement. A step up in trip to two and a half miles will help at some point."

Novice: Windbeneathmywings (b120): "Recovered from his setback, has summered well and literally could be anything."

Dan Skelton

Wins-Runs in Britain in 2024/25	**179-996**
Highest-rated horse in training	**Grey Dawning** Timeform Rating c164

Chaser: Grey Dawning (c164): "He was unlucky last year not to win the Betfair Chase as when it rained all day the rain probably just gave the advantage to our opposition. Hopefully we have him in similar form and everything goes swimmingly through the autumn, and we can go back there."

Hurdler: The New Lion (h161p): "He had a great year as a novice, and we are going to come back in trip and head down the Champion Hurdle route. We will aim to start at the Fighting Fifth. He has had a great summer and looks fantastic."

Novice: Mydaddypaddy (b109p): "He looked very good winning his bumper at Huntingdon. He is only a four-year-old, but we like everything we have seen and hope that he will be a very progressive novice hurdler."

Jamie Snowden

Wins-Runs in Britain in 2024/25	**62-294**
Highest-rated horse in training	**Datsalrightgino** Timeform Rating c157

Chaser: Wendigo (h136): "He won an Irish point for Colin Bowe as a four-year-old and won two bumpers for us. He won a Class 3 novice hurdle in the autumn and ran a fine race to be second in the Grade 1 Challow behind the subsequent Turners winner. He defied a penalty when winning at Wetherby before he was fifth in the Grade 1 Albert Bartlett at the Cheltenham Festival, where he was arguably very unlucky. He'll go novice chasing this season and has the potential to be very smart."

Hurdler: Tiptoptim (b94): "Out of an unraced Sir Percy mare who was the half-sister to the Grade 1 winner Grumeti and the seven-time winner Ellerslie Tom. Tiptoptim won an Irish point for Monbeg stables. He was a really pleasing third on his racecourse debut in a bumper at Plumpton and improved for the outing to win well on his next start. He jumps well and can develop into a smart novice hurdler."

Novice: Senator (Unraced over jumps): "By Doctor Dino (the sire of multiple Grade 1 winners including State Man, Sharjah and Sceau Royal) out of a five-time winning Martaline mare, who was a listed jumps winner at Auteuil. The pedigree is packed full of black-type jumpers including Grade 1 winning juvenile hurdler Porticello. Senator was third in two Flat races this spring at around a mile and a half, on each occasion staying on strongly inside the final furlong. He is bred to jump and was taking on Flat-bred individuals which makes his performances even better. He has schooled well over hurdles and looks a seriously smart juvenile hurdle prospect for the winter. He should be one for the Triumph Hurdle at the Cheltenham Festival, whilst he might be one for the Ascot Stakes at Royal Ascot next summer."

RISING STARS

Dylan Johnston

Attached Stable	**Sam Thomas**
First Ride	**2019**
First Winner	**Willyouwalkwithme** Downpatrick 13/6/2021
Total Winners	**60**
Best Jumps Horses Ridden	**Al Dancer** Timeform Rating c159

Dylan Johnston's 'Rising Star' status was given a boost in the summer of 2024 when the conditional was appointed retained rider to leading owner Dai Walters, whose main trainer Sam Thomas is based in South Wales. Thomas had already used Johnston's valuable 7 lb claim on Iwilldoit when the top weight finished third in the 2023 Welsh Grand National and that led to Johnston partnering Walters' very smart chaser Al Dancer later that season, including when runner-up in the Coral Trophy at Kempton.

Johnston's appointment as retained rider wasn't entirely out of the blue, therefore, and he soon rewarded the decision by winning the Welsh Champion Hurdle last October on Walters' smart hurdler Lump Sum. Johnston later rode the same horse to finish second in the Fighting Fifth Hurdle (when unable to use his claim) and the William Hill Hurdle at Newbury.

Johnston ended last season with a career-best total of 27 winners, with Neil Mulholland, for whom he had an impressive 26% strike rate, providing ten of those winners and Thomas 11.

Dublin-born Johnston had started off as a conditional with Stuart Crawford and rode his first winner for fellow Northern Ireland trainer Harry Smyth, one of Rachael Blackmore's early supporters, when Willyouwalkwithme won a handicap hurdle at Downpatrick in 2021. He then moved to Britain, joining Rose Dobbin's Northumberland yard—her husband, Grand National-winning jockey Tony, had made the same move from Northern Ireland to the north of England himself. Johnston's first winner in Britain came at Carlisle on Dobbin's Cliffs of Dooneen in April 2022.

The next chapter in Johnston's progressive career and an important stepping stone to his current role came with a move south to Olly Murphy's yard in the summer of 2023. It wasn't long after his biggest win to date, on Murphy's Pickanumber in the 2024 Swinton Handicap Hurdle at Haydock that May, that he was snapped up by Walters.

Callum Pritchard

Attached Stable	**Ben Pauling**
First Ride	**2023**
First Winner	**Dan's Chosen** Ludlow 26/10/2023
Total Winners	**36**
Best Jumps Horses Ridden	**Al Dancer** Timeform Rating c159

Wales is proving a fertile breeding ground for jump jockeys these days, with Sean Bowen becoming champion for the first time last season and Callum Pritchard finishing runner-up in the conditional jockeys' championship with 32 winners, seven behind one of our Rising Stars from last year Freddie Gingell. In contrast to the latter whose career was already building rapid momentum, Pritchard came from virtually nowhere, having ridden only a single winner from 40 rides under Rules, when still an amateur, prior to last season.

A rugby player in his youth, Pritchard came relatively late to racing, graduating from hunting and then, almost by accident, point-to-points. It was only as a result of his girlfriend's pointer needing a rider that Pritchard took out a licence to ride between the flags, but such was his success in the pointing field that he became champion novice for the 2022/23 season. By then, Pritchard had joined the stable of Philip Hobbs and Johnson White and it was they who supplied that first winner under Rules in October 2023 when Dan's Chosen won an amateur jockeys' handicap chase at Ludlow.

It was to be just over a year before Pritchard doubled his tally under Rules, but in the meantime his stable provided him with a first Cheltenham Festival ride (Celebre d'Allen, who was unlucky to unseat in the Kim Muir).

It was on the suggestion of fellow Welshman Ben Jones, brother of Pritchard's girlfriend Hannah, and who was then already riding for Hobbs and White, that he should join the Somerset yard. Jones then landed the job of stable jockey to Ben Pauling in the autumn of 2024 and enjoyed a hugely successful season himself, while Pritchard had made the same move by the end of the year. However, it was his former yard which provided him with most of last season's winners, three of those coming on useful hurdler Tiny Tetley.

Pritchard's first win for Pauling had come in November on the unpredictable Densworth in a handicap chase at Wetherby. He enjoyed a purple patch that month with ten winners, much the most important of which was Al Dancer's exhilarating victory at 25/1 in the Badger Beer Handicap Chase at Wincanton, just his third winner as a conditional.

Conor Stone-Walsh

Attached Stable	**Gavin Cromwell**
First Ride	**2022 (Flat) 2023 (Jumps)**
First Winner	**Malaysian** Dundalk 02/12/2022
Total Winners	**62 (including 28 on Flat)**
Best Jumps Horses Ridden	**Perceval Legallois** Timeform Rating c158

Jockeys can sometimes become less fashionable and struggle to maintain their success after riding out their claim, but Conor Stone-Walsh's association with the powerful Gavin Cromwell yard should ensure opportunities remain plentiful, despite having to compete on level terms against more established riders. Cromwell finished third in the Irish trainers' championship for the first time ever last season, behind only Willie Mullins and Gordon Elliott, while his tally of 85 winners was a seasonal best. Stone-Walsh was aboard 13 of those winners, including Backtonormal who won a valuable handicap chase at the Dublin Racing Festival and remains one to follow. Other notable winners Stone-Walsh partnered for Cromwell last season included The King of Prs, who won the Dan & Joan Moore Memorial Handicap Chase at Fairyhouse, and Al Gasparo who won a premier handicap hurdle at Leopardstown's Christmas Festival. It's also telling that Stone-Walsh was entrusted with the ride on Thecompanysergeant who was well fancied for the TrustATrader Plate Handicap Chase at the Cheltenham Festival. Neither horse nor rider disappointed on the big stage, but they were unlucky to bump into a rapidly-progressive rival in Jagwar and had to settle for second.

Stone-Walsh has a greater bank of race-riding experience to call on than his record under Rules would suggest having graduated from the famed Irish pony racing circuit. He furthered his education as an apprentice with Joseph O'Brien, riding 28 winners on the Flat before switching his attention to jumps in 2023, rather than facing a prolonged battle with the scales. He didn't have to wait long to reap the rewards for that decision as he was successful in a handicap hurdle at Cork in November on his first ride over jumps, aboard Dgalwaygallivantor for Cromwell. He then won a listed chase at Fairyhouse only six days later, on Solness for O'Brien, on his first ride over fences. Stone-Walsh lost his claim when riding his 60th winner across Flat and jumps aboard CJ's Darling in a maiden hurdle at Sligo in July, and it bodes well for his prospects that Cromwell was still willing to give him rides in the Galway Plate and Galway Hurdle even without his allowance.

Ewan Whillans

Base	**Newmill Stables, Hawick, Scottish Borders**
First Full Licence	**2021**
First winner under Rules	**Cracking Destiny** Stratford 19/08/2021
Total Winners	**87 (including 42 on Flat)**
Best Horse Trained	**Cracking Rhapsody** Timeform Rating h138

It was a case of start as you mean to go on for Ewan Whillans who, after taking over the licence from his father Alistair in the summer of 2021, sent out a 305/1 double with his first couple of runners at Stratford, including 50/1 shot Scots Poet in the concluding bumper. Whillans' first winner was provided by Cracking Destiny, the older half-brother to the horse who has developed into the yard's flagbearer, Cracking Rhapsody.

Cracking Rhapsody has proved a fine advertisement for his trainer's talent since winning a Perth bumper in the summer of 2023 on his second start, and he won three times during his first campaign over hurdles in the 2023/24 season, most notably the valuable Morebattle at Kelso, before signing off with a close-up third in the Scottish Champion Hurdle at Ayr. Cracking Rhapsody understandably rose in the weights and ended the season rated a full stone higher with the BHA than when runner-up on his handicap debut at Kelso, but Whillans managed to coax further improvement from his stable star last term and he enjoyed another terrific campaign. The Morebattle Hurdle again featured among Cracking Rhapsody's three wins for the season, but so too did the Scottish Champion Hurdle, in which he showed a tremendous attitude to prevail in a blanket finish.

Cracking Rhapsody has perhaps been underestimated during his career—as demonstrated by last season's Morebattle and Scottish Champion Hurdle victories coming at double-figure prices—and the same is true of Whillans who shows a healthy level-stakes profit with his hurdlers. Backing each of his 259 runners over hurdles would have resulted in 29 winners for a profit of £103.82 to £1 level stakes. Luminaries, who rattled off a quickfire hat-trick at Newcastle in the spring, was another to contribute towards Whillans' 15 winners for the season, which represents the trainer's best campaign yet over jumps. The dual-purpose Whillans has also been experiencing a fruitful time of things on the Flat in 2025 and by the end of June had already set a new seasonal best tally. He can continue on the upward curve during the jumps season.

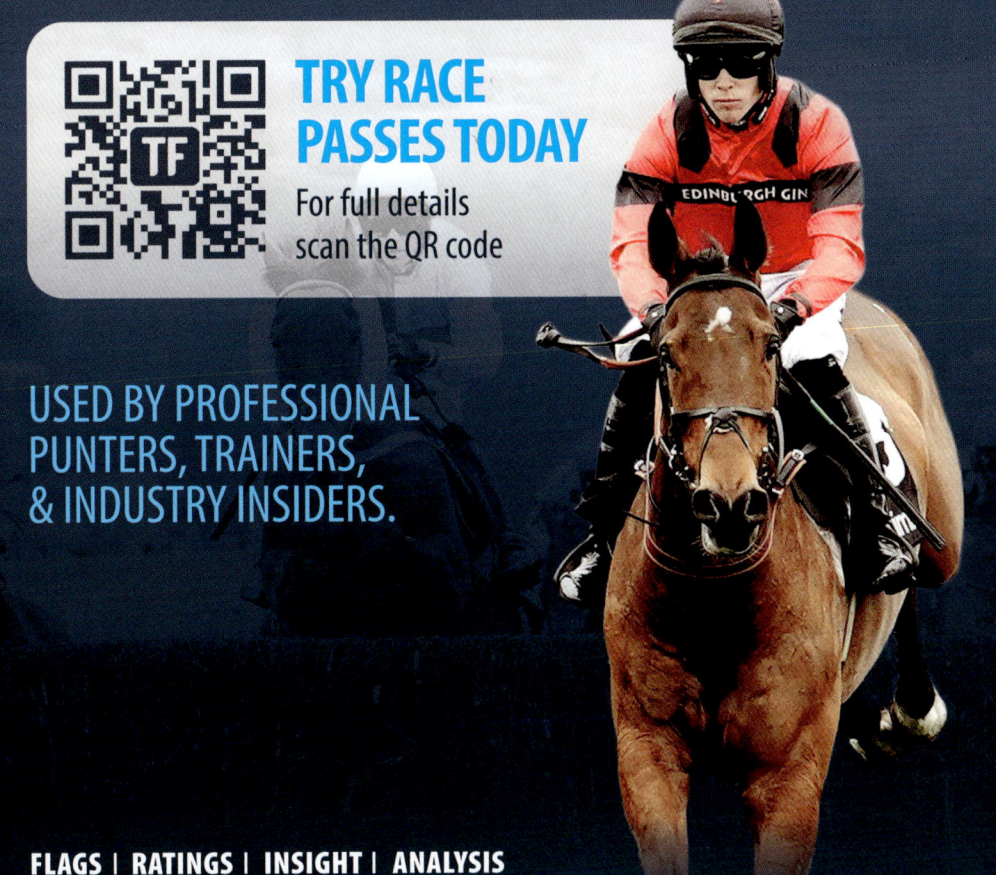

STABLE SWITCHERS

John Ingles highlights ten horses that have moved yards and will be worth noting.

A Moments Madness (Ire)   h104 c113
6 b.g. Conduit (Ire) – Miss Sarenne (Fr) (Robin des Pres (Fr))

A Moments Madness, trained by Warren Greatrex, was among the Million In Mind Partnership's latest draft at the Goffs UK Spring Horses In Training Sales at Doncaster and will be continuing his career for Fergal O'Brien who was the successful bidder at £82,000. The six-year-old didn't make his Rules debut until last autumn and was then switched to fences mid-way through the season, meaning that he's lightly raced overall but particularly unexposed as a chaser. A Moments Madness made the frame in all his completed starts, and while he showed ability over hurdles, his form improved over the larger obstacles. Returning from a breathing operation in the spring, A Moments Madness was second at Fontwell before going one better in a handicap at Ffos Las on his final start which he won with something in hand after making all the running. A lengthy gelding who was runner-up in an Irish point, A Moments Madness will stay beyond two and a half miles and gives the impression there could be more to come. *Fergal O'Brien*

Gold Cast (Fr)   h110p
3 b.f. Telecaster – Shannon Marigold (Fr) (Martaline)

Gold Cast is one of two big-money purchases, both three-year-olds, to have joined Paul Nicholls from the Arqana Deauville Summer Sale. From the first crop of Dante Stakes winner Telecaster, Gold Cast was bought for €300,000, with some of Nicholls' owners apparently banding together to see off interest from Willie Mullins. Gold Cast had three runs over hurdles at Auteuil in April/May for Mickael Seror. Fitted with a hood for her debut only, she progressed with each run and got her head in front on her final start with a game effort to win by a short neck. Bryony Frost was in the saddle for Gold Cast's last two runs and was no doubt able to give a favourable report on the filly before the sale to her former boss. Gold Cast is out of a sister to Shannon Rock, a very smart if rather frustrating chaser who was runner-up four times in the Grand Steeple-Chase de Paris, so she's sure to stay further than two miles in due course. *Paul Nicholls*

Kingston Pride (Ire)   h127
6 gr.g. Kingston Hill – Milans Pride (Ire) (Milan)

For the second time in his life, Kingston Pride changed hands for a lot of money when he was bought at the Goffs UK Spring Sale in May. He had already been sold for €200,000 as a four-year-old after winning his sole outing in Irish points and has now joined Olly Murphy for £285,000 after showing plenty of promise in just a handful of

Kingston Pride is still lightly raced and could have more to offer

starts for Nicky Henderson. Kingston Pride had two runs in bumpers early in 2024, finishing second to Tripoli Flyer, who was subsequently runner-up in a Grade 2 at Aintree, on his debut at Lingfield before winning readily at Exeter. Switched to hurdles last season, he created a fine impression when winning a maiden at Uttoxeter with plenty in hand, though seemed not to handle softer ground when pulled up in the Winter Novices' Hurdle at Sandown for which he started the 6/4 favourite. However, he got back on track on better ground in the spring in a novice at Kempton when beating Paul Nicholls' Winter Novices' runner-up Quebecois in what was a virtual match. From the family of Hennessy Gold Cup winner Trabolgan, Kingston Pride should make a useful novice chaser for his new connections. *Olly Murphy*

Macao (Fr)   b103
3 ch.g. Telecaster – Cour d'Eau Ludique (Fr) (Barastraight)

French imports have been integral to Venetia Williams' success over the years and Macao must rate as one of the yard's most expensive recruits after being bought for €320,000 at the Arqana Deauville Summer Sale. By the same sire as Gold Cast, Telecaster, the non-thoroughbred Macao is from a successful jumping family, with his dam being a sister to Baie des Iles, a useful chaser who gained a notable success at Auteuil in the Prix des Drags during her time with Irish trainer Ross O'Sullivan.

Macao won his only start in France for Henri-Francois Devin, facing just three rivals in a bumper at Lyon Parilly in June. While he had the run of the race, dictating a steady pace, and showed signs of inexperience, he quickened in good style in the straight to pull six lengths clear at the line. There's more substance to that form than might be imagined, though, as runner-up Mysoko Star went on to win a Group 3 bumper at Vichy later in the summer. *Venetia Williams*

Narciso Has (Fr) h123p
3 b.g. Doctor Dino (Fr) – Chegei Has (Fr) (Kahyasi)

The Prix Wild Monarch, a race for three-year-old newcomers and run at Auteuil in April, has been the starting point for some very successful jumping careers in recent seasons. In 2023, for example, it was fought out by Sir Gino and Salvator Mundi, the latter going on to win the latest edition of the Top Novices' Hurdle for Willie Mullins. State Man and Gaelic Warrior are others to have started out in the Wild Monarch before joining Mullins and the latest winner, Narciso Has, is another to have found his way to Closutton. Trained by Marcel Rolland and wearing a tongue tie, Narciso Has jumped well in a share of the lead with eventual runner-up Diabolo Vert before asserting late to win by a length and a quarter. Narciso Has is by State Man's sire Doctor Dino and he's out of Chegei Has who was smart at her best over hurdles in France and a useful chaser. Narciso Has was bought privately for JP McManus and he'll no doubt be campaigned with the Triumph Hurdle in mind. *Willie Mullins*

Nativehill (Ire) h109
7 b.g. Flemensfirth (USA) – Fairy Native (Ire) (Be My Native (USA))

Nativehill was another purchase by Fergal O'Brien at Doncaster in May and at £45,000 he could prove well bought. After all, he'd topped the Goffs UK Aintree Sale in 2023 when selling for £260,000 after winning the second of his Irish points and had just three starts over hurdles for Nicky Henderson last season. After being promoted a place when third past the post on his debut at Newbury last December, Nativehill was tongue tied for the first time when landing the odds in workmanlike fashion in a maiden hurdle at Huntingdon in early-March after being left clear at the last. It had evidently been something of a rush to get him ready to carry the sponsors' colours in the Albert Bartlett Novices' Hurdle, but he took his chance as a 66/1 shot at Cheltenham just 12 days later. Predictably, he found it all too much and was tailed off when pulled up. But the strong, lengthy Nativehill is every inch a chaser on looks and will surely prove a different proposition given a stamina test over fences; his half-brothers include Bellshill, winner of the Punchestown and Irish Gold Cups. *Fergal O'Brien*

Poetisa (Ire)   b91
4 b.f. Poet's Word (Ire) – Chars (Ire) (Old Vic)

Most of Willie Mullins' new recruits this season have been bought privately in France, but Poetisa went through the ring at Doncaster in May and at £300,000 was the most expensive lot at the Spring Horses In Training Sale. Poetisa was sent off at 20/1 for her debut in the mares' bumper at Cheltenham's April meeting but overcame a troubled run in a messy race to make a winning debut for Lambourn trainer Toby Bulgin. After not getting a clear run over two furlongs out, Poetisa improved to lead in the final furlong and kept on to win by a neck and three quarters of a length from fellow newcomers Noble Grace and Sheezer Dancer. Poetisa is by King George winner Poet's Word and a half-sister to Queenohearts who was herself a listed bumper winner before making into a useful hurdler who stayed three miles. Her dam is an unraced half-sister to high-class Irish hurdler Macs Joy. Mullins got the better of Nicky Henderson to secure Poetisa who will race for Gigginstown House Stud. *Willie Mullins*

Pourquoi Pas Papa (Fr)   h123p
3 b.g. Manatee – Pourquoi Pas Elle (Fr) (Martaline)

Pourquoi Pas Papa was Paul Nicholls' other big-money buy at Deauville in July when selling for €200,000. He had made his debut at Clairefontaine the previous month for David Cottin in a hurdle for unraced three-year-olds and showed plenty of promise in finishing a length and a half second to Parchment. Jumping well in a share of the lead for a long way, Pourquoi Pas Papa couldn't quicken initially after the last but was keeping on well again at the finish. Bidding on behalf of Nicholls, Anthony Bromley recalled that he had bought the 2015 Triumph Hurdle winner Peace And Co after winning the same Clairefontaine race earlier that season. Pourquoi Pas Papa is by Manatee, a very smart performer up to 15 furlongs in France and out of Pourquoi Pas Elle who won a cross-country chase at Pau and has bred a couple of winning jumpers in France. This is also the family of Toubab who was a smart chaser when trained by Nicholls, finishing second to Sprinter Sacre in the Maghull Novices' Chase. *Paul Nicholls*

Push The Button (Ire)   h134
6 gr.g. Kingston Hill – Tara Rose (Kayf Tara)

North Yorkshire trainer Mark Walford has some promising types for novice chases among the *Fifty* and may well have acquired another with the purchase for £105,000 of Push The Button out of Nigel Twiston-Davies' stable at Doncaster in May. Push The Button won a bumper for his previous yard and two of his three runs the following season in a curtailed novice hurdle campaign. While he failed to get his head in front last term, Push The Button was only beaten a head when wearing cheekpieces for the first time in a competitive handicap at Windsor in January. The headgear was retained for his remaining starts, and after getting badly hampered at the start when sixth in the

Push The Button (grey) was only narrowly beaten at Windsor and should make a chaser for his new yard

Martin Pipe at the Festival, Push The Button filled the same spot in a premier handicap at Aintree. A strong gelding by Kingston Pride's sire Kingston Hill, Push The Button is a chasing type on looks. He stays three miles and acts on heavy ground though doesn't necessarily need the mud. *Mark Walford*

Zekret (Fr)   f100
3 ch.c. Zarak (Fr) – Anjella (Ger) (Monsun (Ger))

After showing useful form for Andre Fabre on the Flat, Zekret was the top lot to change hands by some way at the Deauville Summer Sale. While this was another one that got away as far as team Mullins was concerned, Zekret, still an entire at the time of his sale, was still destined for Ireland as he has joined Joseph O'Brien for €520,000. Zekret raced only four times for Al Shaqab, winning his only outing at two at Deauville, and on his final start in France was only beaten around three lengths into fifth in the Group 3 Prix Hocquart over 11 furlongs at Longchamp in May. His sire Zarak is doing well under both codes, with his best hurdler being the smart Zarak The Brave, winner of the Galway Hurdle for Mullins. Zekret comes from a very successful German family that includes the Melbourne Cup winner Almandin, but it has thrown up a high-class hurdler, too, in Aramon who was an earlier Galway Hurdle winner for Mullins. *Joseph O'Brien*

HORSES TO FOLLOW

ANTE-POST BETTING

Timeform's Andrew Asquith looks at the markets for some of the highlights in the National Hunt calendar and picks out his best value bets...

King George VI Chase

The King George VI was an atypical renewal last season, featuring a double-figure field for the first time since 2018 courtesy of a strong Irish and French challenge, while it also lacked a standout performer. It was won by the Joseph O'Brien-trained **Banbridge**, who came out on top from **Il Est Francais** in a thrilling finish. From a form perspective, it was the best renewal since Cue Card edged out Vautour in the 2015 edition, so both need respecting this time around even though they disappointed in the spring. Banbridge had a lot in his favour that day, though, and you could argue Il

The Jukebox Man impressed when landing the Kauto Star Novices' Chase at Kempton

Est Francais failed to get home under a very positive ride. **Gaelic Warrior** heads the ante-post market at the time of writing, and three miles around Kempton should be perfect for him, but connections weren't tempted last year, and playing Willie Mullins roulette is a dangerous game this far out. He is easy enough to pass over at the prices with that in mind, and it could be the year for one of last season's top novices to break through in the King George. **The Jukebox Man** had his novice season cut short after suffering an injury on the gallops, but he had looked a potential top-notcher prior to that, unbeaten in two starts and bagging a Grade 1 on just his second appearance over fences in the Kauto Star Novices' Chase, run over the same course and distance as the King George. Admittedly, it wasn't the deepest renewal—there were only five runners and The Jukebox Man started as the 4/6 favourite—but he dispatched some lesser rivals in the exact fashion you would have expected, and he was one of the ante-post favourites for the Brown Advisory Novices' Chase at the Cheltenham Festival after crossing the line. **Lecky Watson** didn't need to run to a much higher level to win the Brown Advisory, and he probably would have had his work cut out with Ben Pauling's unexposed seven-year-old had he been fit and able to compete. Pauling sees The Jukebox Man as a potential Gold Cup horse this season and, given he's on course to return in the autumn, the King George will likely be his main early-season target. Prices around 16/1 look too big for a horse of his potential.

SELECTION: The Jukebox Man (16/1)

Champion Hurdle

Last season's Champion Hurdle had the potential for one of the market principals to record one of the great hurdling performances of recent years, with **Constitution Hill** going up against progressive mare **Brighterdaysahead** and 2024 winner **State Man**, but what transpired was far from the case. Constitution Hill was still travelling powerfully when departing at the fifth flight, and State Man was around five lengths clear when falling at the last, while Brighterdaysahead ran below form to leave 25/1 shot Golden Ace to prevail. She earned the lowest rating for a Champion Hurdle winner this century, by some margin, and it will be an even bigger surprise if she's able to follow up this season. There is new blood in the division this time around and The New Lion looks a bona-fide Champion Hurdle contender. He went from strength to strength last season and his unbeaten campaign, featuring four wins at trips around two and a half miles, culminated with a high-class effort in the Grade 1 Turners Novices' Hurdle at the Cheltenham Festival. The New Lion put some other exciting novices to the sword that day, showing significant improvement to beat the pick of the Irish challenge in determined fashion. He is yet to race over two miles over hurdles, but you need to stay well to win a Champion Hurdle, and the manner he travels through his races suggests the shorter trip won't pose a problem. Trainer Dan Skelton has already outlined he will be campaigned with the Champion Hurdle in mind, and he deserves his place at the head of the market given he's the rising force in the division and doesn't have much to find on form with State Man and Lossiemouth.

SELECTION: The New Lion (9/2)

Queen Mother Champion Chase

Marine Nationale was a good winner of the Champion Chase last season for this section, but, a bit like the Champion Hurdle, the race didn't go to script as odds-on favourite **Jonbon** made a jolting mistake at the ninth that effectively ended his chance. Marine Nationale was 14/1 when selected this time last year and he's now only 5/1. Admittedly, he did back his Cheltenham performance up at Punchestown the following month, but there are some exciting novices from last season who have the potential to improve past him. The Nicky Henderson-trained Sir Gino tops the betting and it is easy to see why given the impression he made on his sole start over fences when beating Ballyburn in the Wayward Lad Novices' Chase at Kempton. He was ruled out for the rest of the season with an infection, but he is back at Seven Barrows and remains a top-class prospect. However, his price is probably about right. With doubts about **Majborough**'s jumping, and the potential that he might be upped in trip for the Ryanair, it is the Paul Nicholls-trained **Kalif du Berlais** who makes most appeal at the prices. He was impressive when winning the Maghull Novices' Chase at Aintree on his final start, jumping in exemplary fashion and travelling through the race like a

Kalif du Berlais signed off for the season with a Grade 1 victory in the Maghull Novices' Chase

horse who is capable of posting a higher figure when the time demands it. He won a handicap at Cheltenham with ease before that, so the track clearly will be no issue, and you need a horse who can travel and jump well in a Champion Chase. Odds of 16/1 more than likely underestimate his chance, and you would imagine he'll be well placed to pick up some races prior to March so should shorten in the betting.

SELECTION: Kalif du Berlais (16/1)

Stayers' Hurdle

The Stayers' division has been open for a while now, and it remains that way heading into this season. **Teahupoo** won the Stayers' in 2024 and started a strong favourite last season but, though he did little wrong, he was unable to repel the challenge of **Bob Olinger**, who arrived travelling well and found more than he had done previously when push came to shove. Bob Olinger will be an 11-year-old next year, though, while Teahupoo's level of form doesn't set too high a standard. Therefore, this season's renewal of the Stayers' looks set for a younger horse to come through the ranks, and **Jasmin de Vaux** has all the right credentials to do so. He went from strength to strength over hurdles last season, dismissing a couple of below-par efforts in Grade 1s over shorter when winning the Albert Bartlett at the Cheltenham Festival where he relished the extra emphasis on stamina. Jasmin de Vaux did especially well

Jasmin de Vaux improved when upped in trip for the Albert Bartlett Novices' Hurdle

to follow up at the Punchestown Festival on his final start given jockey Paul Townend crossed the line with his feet out of the irons after losing them following an awkward landing at the last. Jasmin de Vaux showed a nice blend of speed and stamina at Punchestown to beat another progressive type who had missed Cheltenham, and he could dominate this division for seasons to come being only a six-year-old. Jasmin de Vaux isn't the most imposing type, so you would imagine his future lies over hurdles, especially given Willie Mullins has Final Demand for staying novice chases this season.

SELECTION: Jasmin de Vaux (8/1)

Cheltenham Gold Cup

Only nine runners went to post for the Gold Cup last season, the joint-smallest field in the 2000s, but no obvious contenders were missing, and there don't appear to be many potential top-class, staying chasers coming through the ranks. Therefore, it could well be another small-field Gold Cup this season and there is no urge to oppose reigning champion **Inothewayurthinkin**. He started 13/8 favourite when winning the Kim Muir in imperious fashion at the 2024 Cheltenham Festival and he looked excellent once more when stretching six lengths clear in the Gold Cup last

Inothewayurthinkin was a dominant winner of the Cheltenham Gold Cup

season, denying **Galopin des Champs** a famous hat-trick. Inothewayurthinkin had been beaten by Galopin des Champs on his previous two starts, but he relished the return to Cheltenham and longer distance of the Gold Cup, producing a top-class display and running to a level not far behind the pick of Galopin des Champs' form. Inothewayurthinkin was installed a short-priced favourite for the Grand National in the immediate aftermath, but connections wisely didn't go to Aintree, probably mindful that they have age on their side and more Gold Cups to win. Inothewayurthinkin will only be an eight-year-old next March, whereas Galopin des Champs and **Fastorslow** will both be ten, while **Fact To File** may well head back to the Ryanair. Serious competition could be thin on the ground and, therefore, odds of 4/1 make appeal for a horse with Inothewayurthinkin's profile and unbeaten Cheltenham record.

SELECTION: Inothewayurthinkin (4/1)

Grand National

Willie Mullins saddled five of the first seven home in the 2025 Grand National, a rare feat even for a powerhouse trainer, with **Nick Rockett** leading home 2024 winner **I Am Maximus** and **Grangeclare West** in third. **Iroko**, who finished fourth, had clearly been campaigned with the Grand National in mind and will surely be a force once more for his burgeoning yard. However, looking at the betting, it is Grangeclare West who is probably a bit too big at 33/1. He started the same price for the latest renewal but he arguably shaped best of all, and his form when splitting Galopin des Champ and Fact To File in the Irish Gold Cup is right up there. He had flopped at Navan, in the Webster Cup, but was freshened up and took to the National fences very well, while also looking a dour stayer. His sole blunder at the final fence arguably cost him his winning chance, but it is testament to his ability and attitude that he came back for more on the run-in, getting to within half a length of stablemate I Am Maximus and three lengths of the winner. Grangeclare West must have come out of the race well as he went to Sandown for the bet365 Gold Cup only three weeks later and ran just as well in fifth. He will be a ten-year-old by the time the Grand National comes around next year, but he's relatively lightly raced for his age, particularly at marathon trips, and will likely be campaigned with Aintree in mind. He represents an all-conquering yard that has won the last two renewals and, given how well he took to the test last season, he's likely to be in the mix.

SELECTION: Grangeclare West (33/1)

SECTION 4

TIMEFORM'S VIEW	104
2024/25 STATISTICS (BRITAIN)	130

TIMEFORM'S VIEW

Chosen from the Timeform formbook, here is Timeform's detailed analysis— compiled by our team of race reporters—of a selection of key races from Cheltenham.

CHELTENHAM Tuesday March 11
GOOD TO SOFT

Michael O'Sullivan Supreme Novices' Hurdle (Grade 1) (1)

Pos	Btn	Horse	Age	Wgt	Eq	Trainer	Jockey	SP
1		KOPEK DES BORDES (FR)	5	11-7	(h)	W. P. Mullins, Ireland	P. Townend	4/6f
2	1¾	WILLIAM MUNNY (IRE)	7	11-7	(h)	Barry Connell, Ireland	Sean Flanagan	8/1
3	5½	ROMEO COOLIO	6	11-7		Gordon Elliott, Ireland	J. W. Kennedy	9/2
4	3¾	KARNIQUET (FR)	5	11-7	(h)	W. P. Mullins, Ireland	D. E. Mullins	33/1
5	7½	SALVATOR MUNDI (FR)	5	11-7	(h+t)	W. P. Mullins, Ireland	Mr P. W. Mullins	14/1
6	9	TUTTI QUANTI (FR)	5	11-7		Paul Nicholls	Harry Cobden	125/1
7	5	IRANCY (FR)	7	11-7		W. P. Mullins, Ireland	M. P. Walsh	25/1
8	½	SKY LORD	6	11-7		Henry de Bromhead, Ireland	D. J. O'Keeffe	50/1
9	12	FUNICULI FUNICULA (FR)	5	11-7		W. P. Mullins, Ireland	B. Hayes	80/1
10	12	KARBAU (FR)	5	11-7		W. P. Mullins, Ireland	S. F. O'Keeffe	40/1
11	14	WORKAHEAD (IRE)	7	11-7		Henry de Bromhead, Ireland	Rachael Blackmore	15/2

11 ran   Race Time 3m 52.80   Closing Sectional (4.10f): 59.4s (97.9%)   Winning Owner: Monabeg Investments Limited

A Supreme named in memory of Michael O'Sullivan, who lost his life after a fall at Thurles last month, a jockey who gained one of his most notable wins aboard Marine Nationale in the 2023 running of this race; a field of 11 went to post this year and the make-up was a fine snapshot of the state of jump racing at present, 6 of the 11 trained by Willie Mullins and the sole British-trained representative the 125/1 complete outsider though the form looks well up to scratch for the race, even if not quite in the league of Constitution Hill or Altior among recent winners; it was well run, the overall time and sectionals supporting a positive view of the form. **Kopek des Bordes** in a first-time hood and reasonably calm in the preliminaries, had to work to maintain his unbeaten record, still something of a work in progress despite the high level of his form, taking a while to settle (helped by the good pace) and his jumping largely only adequate (not so slick as Romeo Coolio in front of him) even before a fluff at the last gave the runner-up half a chance, tracked pace, went with zest, upsides 2 out, went on soon after, quickened straight, not fluent last, ridden out; he's open to further improvement over hurdles, and has the physique to make a chaser, where he goes next season perhaps dependent on the other pieces in the Mullins jigsaw. **William Munny** isn't the most imposing of these, just medium sized, and is older than a typical Supreme candidate, but he's taken well to hurdling and, in a first-time hood, found significant improvement in this higher grade, proving the most serious threat to the winner, even if the way the race developed played to his strengths; patiently ridden, good progress fifth, shaken up after 2 out, went second early in straight, kept on run-in; he's likely to make an impact in good open company over hurdles next winter. **Romeo Coolio** runner-up in the Champion Bumper last season, was placed again at the Festival, continuing his fine start over hurdles, just lacking a turn of foot and looking ready for a step up in trip; tracked pace, travelled well, jumped on fifth, joined 2 out, shaken up, not quicken straight; has done well physically and has all the makings of a good novice chase prospect for next season. **Karniquet** about the pick of the Mullins' runners on looks (though fussy beforehand in hood first time), had been no match for the winner last time and couldn't land a blow on him here either, but he showed further improvement and has the makings of a smashing novice chaser next season; waited with, shaken up before 3 out, not fluent there, ridden after, kept on straight, edged left, made little impression. **Salvator Mundi** went a place better than he had in the Triumph last season, improving a bit on that effort as well, though never posing much of a threat, despite being ridden off the pace, in a similar position to the runner-up; held up, not settle fully, plenty to do 3 out, shaken up after, kept on straight, made little impression. **Tutti Quanti** the sole British-trained runner and with lots to find on form, ran about as well as could have been expected upped in grade, ridden to pick up the pieces and passing beaten horses in the straight without being subjected to a hard race; in rear, lost touch third, tailed off still 2 out, kept on straight without being unduly punished, never nearer; he has the physique to make a better chaser, definitely of interest at that discipline next winter. **Irancy** was below form after 4 months off, perhaps needing the run; soon steadied, not fluent first, hampered before 3 out, shaken up after, one paced straight; he'd looked an exciting prospect in winning at Punchestown and still has longer distances to try, so he remains with some potential. **Sky Lord** had plenty to find on the form he'd shown on his first 2 starts over hurdles and he failed to even match those efforts away from testing ground, not looking entirely straightforward under pressure (in a red hood and on toes beforehand); mid-division, labouring halfway, headway when mistake 3 out, left behind and carried head bit awkwardly from next. **Funiculi Funicula** had won a maiden by a wide margin on his Irish debut, but he was the stable's sixth string judged on the market and never got remotely competitive, likely to benefit from a return to calmer waters; held up, not fluent third, pushed along halfway, behind when mistake 2 out. **Karbau** up significantly in grade, looked out of place in this field beforehand and finished well held, a long way below the useful form he'd shown on heavy ground at Punchestown; in touch, not fluent fourth, lost place soon after, hampered before 3 out, tailed off. **Workahead** had beaten William Munny in landing a maiden when last seen over Christmas and it may be that all wasn't well, his rider reporting that he stopped quickly; led, took keen hold, headed when not fluent fifth, lost place soon after, tailed off when eased after 3 out; it's possibly best to put a line through this run, and he remains with potential.

My Pension Expert Arkle Challenge Trophy Novices' Chase (Grade 1) (1)

Pos	Btn	Horse	Age	Wgt	Eq	Trainer	Jockey	SP
1		JANGO BAIE (FR)	6	11-7		Nicky Henderson	Nico de Boinville	5/1
2	¾	ONLY BY NIGHT (IRE)	7	11-0		Gavin Patrick Cromwell, Ireland	Keith Donoghue	25/1
3	sh	MAJBOROUGH (FR)	5	11-7		W. P. Mullins, Ireland	M. P. Walsh	1/2f
4	¾	L'EAU DU SUD (FR)	7	11-7	(t)	Dan Skelton	Harry Skelton	5/1
5	54	TOUCH ME NOT (IRE)	6	11-7		Gordon Elliott, Ireland	J. W. Kennedy	16/1

5 ran Race Time 3m 54.00 Closing Sectional (3.75f): 54.7s (100.9%) Winning Owner: Countrywide Park Homes Ltd

Sir Gino being on the sidelines might have left a big hole in the 2-mile novice chase division but his absence made for a compelling Arkle as it turned out, cracks in each of the contenders beginning to reveal themselves one by one in a strongly-run race resulting in a finish reminiscent of Champ's RSA as another Henderson-trained novice charged home for a victory that looked most unlikely from a long way out and even as close to home as the last, his surge as others started to gasp for air taking him from fourth to the front in a matter of strides late on. **Jango Baie** spent most of the race looking like a stayer against 2-milers only to charge home and take advantage of his rivals' shortcomings, chiefly jumping ones from the favourite, landing a most unlikely looking success; having led until the third, he dropped to the rear when not fluent at the eighth, was outpaced in last after 4 out and the game looked up when blundering at the next, not fluent again 2 out but soon beginning to engage top gear and finding plenty to take 3 places—and the prize—close home; he's still lightly raced, particularly as a chaser, but if he's to better this form it will surely be back over further. **Only By Night** might have lost her unbeaten record over fences but certainly bolstered her reputation, unconsidered in the betting but spending much of the run-in looking like causing a big surprise; held up, progress after 3 out, produced to lead soon after last, edged out late on. **Majborough** bidding to become the first 5-y-o winner since Voy Por Ustedes in 2006, stood out on form in the absence of Sir Gino but became the first odds-on shot to be turned over in the Arkle since Sybillin filled the same spot in 1993 (ironically also behind a Henderson-trained horse, Travado), 7 horses having landed the odds since then; his jumping had been scruffy on occasions at Leopardstown and undoubtedly cost him here, brave at several fences upon taking over at the fifth before hitting 4 out with the worst still to come, his chance looking gone when all but coming down 2 out but, to his great credit, despite not being fluent again at the last, rallying well, just about nosing back to the front briefly late on before having to settle for third; to go so close having lost so much ground and momentum with his blunder suggests he's still much the best prospect in this field if his jumping technique can be polished up. **L'Eau du Sud** arrived with an unblemished record over fences but, while running well on form, conspired to finish fourth having looked poised to take advantage of the favourite's race-costing blunder, unfair to say it was a tame finish but others certainly saw it out better, likely to prove best with the emphasis firmly on speed; waited with, not fluent fifth, took second 3 out, left in front next, headed soon after last, no extra late on. **Touch Me Not** in a red hood and a bit fussy in the preliminaries, had chased home Majborough and L'Eau du Sud on his last 2 starts but didn't get near them this time, just not running his race at all having struggled to get into his usual rhythm; led third until untidy and out to his right fifth, pressed leader after, lost ground when jumped right again 3 out, dropped away; he's still rather unfurnished and may yet take his form up a notch over longer trips in time.

Close Brothers Mares' Hurdle (David Nicholson) (Grade 1) (1)

Pos	Btn	Horse	Age	Wgt	Eq	Trainer	Jockey	SP
1		LOSSIEMOUTH (FR)	6	11-5		W. P. Mullins, Ireland	P. Townend	4/6f
2	7½	JADE DE GRUGY (FR)	6	11-5		W. P. Mullins, Ireland	D. E. Mullins	5/1
3	1¾	TAKE NO CHANCES (IRE)	7	11-5		Dan Skelton	Harry Skelton	22/1
4	1½	JETARA (IRE)	7	11-5	(s)	Mrs J. Harrington, Ireland	Sam Ewing	33/1
5	2	JULY FLOWER (FR)	6	11-5		Henry de Bromhead, Ireland	Rachael Blackmore	8/1
6	½	JOYEUSE (FR)	6	11-5		Nicky Henderson	Nico de Boinville	12/1
7	4¾	KALA CONTI (FR)	5	11-5		Gordon Elliott, Ireland	J. W. Kennedy	16/1
8	¾	DYSART ENOS (IRE)	7	11-5		Fergal O'Brien	Jonathan Burke	28/1
9	3¾	QUEENS GAMBLE (IRE)	7	11-5		Harry Derham	Paul O'Brien	66/1
F		GALA MARCEAU (FR)	6	11-5	(h)	W. P. Mullins, Ireland	B. Hayes	66/1

10 ran Race Time 4m 54.10 Closing Sectional (4.10f): 55.7s (108.7%) Winning Owner: Mrs S. Ricci

Amid the changes that Cheltenham made to the Festival programme as the result of what was widely seen as a problem that needed fixing after last season's Festival, the races for mares remained essentially untouched, this race retaining Grade 1 status despite regular complaints about some of the very best mares taking what is generally a softer option against their own sex, that an issue that drew plenty of comment once again when it was announced that Lossiemouth, bidding for a third successive Festival win, would bid to retain her title in this rather than tackle the Champion Hurdle; her presence made for a rather one-sided renewal, having plenty in hand on form and not needing to run to her best to score as she did in a race that was steadily run, the field well grouped until approaching 3 out; Lossiemouth's best form is superior to that achieved by Golden Ace, which may well mean the issue is raised again, though the defenders of the current status quo should it endure with or without a possible ratings ceiling can point to the positive impact on behaviour caused by the incentive of a Grade 1 target at the Cheltenham Festival and the enhanced mares programme in general_the number of mares in training and the percentage of mares among the horses racing over jumps have increased markedly and Golden Ace's admittedly fortunate success gave mares a fifth win in the Champion Hurdle since this race was raised to a Grade 1 in 2015, after 2 other mares had won the race following the introduction of the mares allowance in 1983/84 and only one at all between 1927 and 1983. **Lossiemouth** taking the easier option, bidding for a repeat win in this race rather than tackle the Champion Hurdle, proved very straightforward as she added a third Festival win to her record, not needing to run to her very best to score with plenty in hand; prominent, took keen hold, led on bridle approaching last, quickened clear, shaken up briefly run-in, impressive; she went on to the Grade 1 at Punchestown after this race last season, and presumably will again, rather than tackle the open Grade 1 at 2m, assuming all is well with State Man. **Jade de Grugy** making a relatively quick return after her reappearance win, couldn't quite match that effort away from soft/heavy ground, setting a stronger gallop perhaps likely to have seen her to better advantage; led, jumped well, shaken up after 2 out, headed entering straight, left behind by winner soon after; she'd looked open to more improvement after her win last time and it is still possible to envisage circumstances in which she will run to a higher rating. **Take No Chances** emerged with plenty of credit upped in grade, understandably unable to land a blow at a pair that were ridden more prominently in a steadily-run race and doing well under the circumstances; held up, ridden before 2 out, headway approaching last, went third there, no further impression. **Jetara** wasn't disgraced, her best efforts generally having come with more emphasis on stamina; prominent, shaken up after 3 out, outpaced home turn, hung left, kept on run-in. **July Flower** on her toes beforehand, was below form, a more steadily-run race than the one she'd won at Leopardstown at Christmas not showing her to best advantage; held up, headway fifth, every chance 2 out, shaken up after, not quicken straight. **Joyeuse** looked open to improvement, but she needed to find quite a bit to be competitive at this level and she wasn't able to, perhaps a steadily-run race (in contrast to Newbury last time) not showing her to advantage, though her jumping wasn't so slick, either; handy, not settle fully, outpaced after 3 out, mistake next, rallied early in straight, disputing fourth when not fluent last, no extra. **Kala Conti** on paper had a similar chance to July Flower on their running at Christmas, but she was sent off at twice the odds and failed to repeat that effort, despite a race that placed relatively little emphasis on stamina; mid-division, effort before 2 out, left behind straight. **Dysart Enos** had had nearly 3 months off since her poor run at Ascot and was back somewhere near her best, facing a very stiff task in this grade, though her stamina for the longer trip is hard to judge conclusively given the grade and the way the race developed; held up, effort 3 out, slow 2 out, left behind soon after. **Queens Gamble** was an optimistic runner at this level and ran below form, though lack of stamina over an extra 2f might also have been a factor; held up, shaken up 3 out, weakened before last. **Gala Marceau** hasn't been near her best in her visits to Britain since finishing runner-up to Lossiemouth in the 2023 Triumph and didn't get the chance to improve on that, her jumping again letting her down; held up, not fluent third, yet to be asked for effort when fell 3 out.

Unibet Champion Hurdle Challenge Trophy (Grade 1) (1)

Pos	Btn	Horse	Age	Wgt	Eq	Trainer	Jockey	SP
1		GOLDEN ACE	7	11-3		Jeremy Scott	Lorcan Williams	25/1
2	9	BURDETT ROAD	5	11-10	(t)	James Owen	Sam Twiston-Davies	66/1
3	1½	WINTER FOG (IRE)	11	11-10		W. P. Mullins, Ireland	B. Hayes	150/1
4	9	BRIGHTERDAYSAHEAD (FR)	6	11-3		Gordon Elliott, Ireland	J. W. Kennedy	5/2
5	10	KING OF KINGSFIELD (IRE)	7	11-10		Gordon Elliott, Ireland	Danny Gilligan	200/1
F		CONSTITUTION HILL	8	11-10		Nicky Henderson	Nico de Boinville	1/2f
F		STATE MAN (FR)	8	11-10	(s)	W. P. Mullins, Ireland	P. Townend	8/1

7 ran Race Time 3m 56.50 Closing Sectional (4.10f): 62.2s (95.1%) Winning Owner: Mr I. F. Gosden

For the third season in succession a single-figure field for the Champion Hurdle, 7 taking part, as in 2023, which had been the smallest number to line up since 1974; on paper, though, this offered plenty, with Constitution Hill bidding to regain the Champion Hurdle crown after missing last season, Brighterdaysahead having shown form good enough to pose a serious threat and last season's winner State Man also with serious claims, raising the possibility that there would be one of the great hurdling performances in the air, though it was thin air as it turned out with 2 of the 3 seeming principals falling—State Man when in command at the last—and the other nowhere near their best, fortunate Golden Ace the longest-priced winner since Hardy Eustace in 2004, her performance recorded by some way the lowest rating for a Champion Hurdle winner this century, with 2 other outsiders chasing her home. **Golden Ace** rewarded connections for their boldness, running here in preference to the Mares Hurdle, and gained a second Festival win with a career-best effort, though her victory owed plenty to fortune and her winning performance rates as one of the lowest in the last 50 years; waited with, hampered fifth, effort when not fluent 3 out, stayed on entering straight, left in front last, kept on well run-in, kept up to work. **Burdett Road** had much the same chance as the winner on their running in the Kingwell and he would have got quite a bit closer to her had he not been badly baulked after the last, though it's doubtful he would have found enough to get to her; dropped out, awkward second, hampered fifth, pushed along 3 out, keeping on when not fluent last, baulked run-in, one paced. **Winter Fog** was essentially out of his depth again, though he picked up place money in a Grade 1 for the fourth time this season, just under £48k here; waited with, labouring 3 out, not fluent 2 out, stayed on straight, hampered last, took third run-in. **Brighterdaysahead** runner-up to Golden Ace in the Dawn Run last season, had since stamped herself as a serious player at the highest level with her 2 Grade 1 wins this winter, but she proved most disappointing, going to the front 3 out seemingly with plenty of running left but already weakening when badly hampered at the last. **King of Kingsfield** acted as the pacemaker for Brighterdaysahead after 10 weeks off and was soon out of contention once his job had been done; led, took keen hold, headed 3 out, soon done with. **Constitution Hill** lost his unbeaten record over hurdles in unexpected fashion, caught out by a hurdle that had been hit by a runner in front of him, after he'd jumped the first 4 in inch-perfect fashion, his style of hurdling a great asset but with little margin for error; he was reportedly none the worse for the experience and hopefully will have an opportunity to show what he can do again this season. **State Man** has a record of durability and consistency, but he was all the sharper for first-time cheekpieces and all set to follow up his win in this race last season when he fell at the last, around 5 lengths up and likely to have won by at least that far, having cruised past Brighterdaysahead soon after 2 out; thankfully, he seemed none the worse for the tumble.

Princess Royal National Hunt Challenge Cup Novices' Handicap Chase (2)

Pos	Btn	Horse	Age	Wgt	Eq	Trainer	Jockey	SP
1		HAITI COULEURS (FR)	8	11-4		Rebecca Curtis	Ben Jones	7/2jf
2	4½	ROCK MY WAY (IRE)	7	11-1	(b+t)	Joe Tizzard	Brendan Powell	16/1
3	1	WILL DO (IRE)	8	11-1	(b)	Gordon Elliott, Ireland	J. W. Kennedy	12/1
4	5½	RESPLENDENT GREY (IRE)	7	11-11		Olly Murphy	Sean Bowen	10/1
5	nk	TRANSMISSION (IRE)	8	11-2	(s)	Neil Mulholland	Mr P. W. Mullins	7/2jf
6	2¾	IN D'OR (FR)	7	11-3		Venetia Williams	Mr David Maxwell	40/1
7	3	HERAKLES WESTWOOD (FR)	8	10-12		Warren Greatrex	Harry Cobden	20/1
8	nk	KLARC KENT (FR)	9	10-10	(s)	W. P. Mullins, Ireland	S. F. O'Keeffe	66/1
9	32	NO TIME TO WAIT (IRE)	7	11-2	(t)	John McConnell, Ireland	D. J. O'Keeffe	33/1
10	8	GERICAULT ROQUE (FR)	9	11-0	(t)	David Pipe	Jack Tudor	11/1
11	30	JUPITER ALLEN (FR)	6	10-7	(s)	Mrs Jane Williams	David Noonan	25/1
F		HASTHING (FR)	8	11-2		Jonjo & A.J. O'Neill	Jonjo O'Neill Jr.	16/1
F		NOW IS THE HOUR (IRE)	8	11-8		Gavin Patrick Cromwell, Ireland	Keith Donoghue	6/1
ur		CAPTAIN CODY (IRE)	7	11-9		W. P. Mullins, Ireland	D. E. Mullins	12/1
bd		DUFFLE COAT (IRE)	8	12-0	(s)	Gordon Elliott, Ireland	Danny Gilligan	50/1
pu		CAESAR ROCK (IRE)	9	10-7	(s)	M. F. Morris, Ireland	Gavin Peter Brouder (3)	80/1
pu		KYNTARA	9	10-8		Mel Rowley	Charlie Deutsch	16/1
pu		STUZZIKINI (IRE)	7	11-9	(b)	Gordon Elliott, Ireland	Sam Ewing	33/1

18 ran Race Time 7m 55.60 Closing Sectional (3.75f): 57.8s (103.2%) Winning Owner: The Brizzle Boys

Positive early signs in terms of improved competitiveness for the first test of the handful of changes to the programme in time for this year's Festival as a race not long prior subjected to a distance tweak attracted a healthy-sized field full of useful novices in its first edition as a handicap open to professional riders; granted it wasn't without its rough and tumble, with a trio set for a frame finish or still in with a chance of one departing in the straight, but it wasn't the last-man-standing test it had become towards the back end of its former days as 'the 4-miler' and the progressive Haiti Couleurs was always well placed in a race that had seen an early dash for the lead soon steady. **Haiti Couleurs** evoked obvious memories of his stable's winning favourite in this Teaforthree from 13 years earlier as he provided his relatively small yard with a sixth Cheltenham Festival winner (first since Lisnagar Oscar in 2020 Stayers' Hurdle), peaking for the day with a spin over hurdles under his belt as he took his form figures since sent chasing to 2111 with yet another fuss-free display, jumping accurately up with the pace (led fifth to eighth and again from 3 out) and yet to be asked for his all a couple of lengths to the good when jumping left into the path of the closing Now Is The Hour who then came to grief, seeing things out well to make sure; he'd have to be high on any shortlist for one of the major staying handicaps at the back end of the season, with the Scottish Grand National a far more compelling option than Sandown given he's been largely kept away from right-handed courses to date. **Rock My Way** seemingly benefited no end from a headgear switch (blinkers instead of cheekpieces) on only his second start for the yard as he acquitted himself with great credit against more than double the number of rivals he'd faced in any of his previous 7 chase starts, looming up soon after 3 out and keeping at it in the winner's wake after Now Is The Hour's fall at the next had left him clear second, the longer trip proving well within range; he's yet to run in an open handicap after plenty of toil so far against unexposed fellow novices. **Will Do** ran at least as well as at Punchestown for all he required the departure of at least one of the others to secure him a fifth placing from 7 starts over fences, during which time he's faced ninety-eight rivals and beaten eighty-one of them despite not yet managing a breakthrough; settled mid-field out wide, effort end of back straight, left clear third at the last, stayed on; he's a likely type for the Irish National. **Resplendent Grey** has displayed greater depths of stamina the more he's raced but also a slovenliness with it which will surely have headgear tried as a potential solution when he's next seen, already losing his mid-field position when wrong at the eighth, behind a circuit out and still labouring in last after 4 out only to pick up so well late on that he was able to capitalise on the mishaps of a few ahead by edging into an unlikely fourth late on. **Transmission** one of only 2 in the field ridden by amateurs in a race now open to professionals, was unable to match previous chasing form here that had been highlighted by a closing second behind Haiti Couleurs (when partnered by the suspended James Bowen) when conceding 2 lb rather than receiving it, firmly up against it under his usual waiting tactics even before a mistake at the eleventh when it became clear the gallop wasn't true, though at least opening up more doors in the end by proving his stamina for a marathon distance as he stayed on gradually in the straight; he's still had a very positive first season over fences and there will be other days for him. **In d'Or** wasn't able to raise his game further but seems likely to do so another day, given he's had only 4 starts over fences and wasn't helped by an early error here; held up, blundered third, crept closer 4 out, shaken up from next, no further impression. **Herakles Westwood** was found out in rather stronger company following a third at Newbury set to be represented later in the week by Lord of Thunder; raced off the pace, hampered seventh, headway under pressure out wide after 3 out, made little impression but didn't shape like a non-stayer upped from 3m. **Klarc Kent** took a much-needed step back in the right direction, though it wasn't pretty even in first-time cheekpieces and he returned last of those not tailed off by the line; close up, lost ground gradually back straight, outpaced before 3 out, plugged on. **No Time To Wait** reverted to looking a clumsy conveyance in a race placing far greater emphasis on his technique; raced off the pace, not jump well, struggling before 4 out. **Gericault Roque** shaped as if retaining plenty of ability this time as well 2 months on from his encouraging belated return only to seem to be totally derailed by an atypical jumping lapse; tracked pace, yet to be asked for effort when clouted 3 out, shaken up after, no response. **Jupiter Allen** found dominating a handicap of this depth well beyond him; made most until 3 out, brushed aside. **Hasthing** met with a fate that ensured he had nothing to show for just how well he'd shaped, doing more to suggest he's still on a mark he can exploit by getting right back into things even after a shocking mistake at the eighteenth, left in a place 2 out and still just about in that position when crumpling to the deck at the last, seemingly tiring at the time over this new trip and likely to have had to settle for fourth at best. **Now Is The Hour** is a must for the shortlist in other big staying handicaps this spring as he'd have finished a fine second at worst in this one—even with only a quartet of maiden runs to his name—had he negotiated 2 out rather than crumpling on landing (winner jumped across him), having closed the gap to just a couple of lengths at the time; he showed over hurdles that stamina is his forte but he's no one-dimensional sluggard judged on how he moved through this under a patient ride. **Captain Cody** had gone the right way in maidens around the turn of the year but seemed to be struggling to hold his mid-field spot in this more competitive environment when unseating at the thirteenth. **Duffle Coat** was in the process of exceeding expectations bearing in mind how many chances he's already had in handicaps when departing; settled in touch (travelled better in refitted cheekpieces), effort approaching straight, keeping on just ahead of Will Do but 4 lengths behind Rock My Way when brought down no sooner than he'd been left in a place 2 out. **Caesar Rock** had been given a break but found the fences getting in the way again; settled in rear out wide, bad mistake seventh, rider lost irons briefly, struggling 4 out; whether he'd benefit from this sort of trip even with a clear round is open to doubt, however. **Kyntara** found this different test all too much thrust into a Festival handicap; handy, lost ground tenth, awkward fourteenth, lost place quickly back straight, pulled up nineteenth. **Stuzzikini** hasn't been near his Troytown form either before or since; mid-field, struggling from 4 out.

CHELTENHAM Wednesday March 12
GOOD TO SOFT

Turners Novices' Hurdle (Baring Bingham) (Grade 1) (1)

Pos	Btn	Horse	Age	Wgt	Eq	Trainer	Jockey	SP
1		THE NEW LION	6	11-7		Dan Skelton	Harry Skelton	3/1
2	¾	THE YELLOW CLAY (IRE)	6	11-7		Gordon Elliott, Ireland	J. W. Kennedy	5/2
3	4¾	FINAL DEMAND (IRE)	6	11-7		W. P. Mullins, Ireland	P. Townend	6/4f
4	9½	FORTY COATS (IRE)	6	11-7		Henry de Bromhead, Ireland	D. J. O'Keeffe	150/1
5	2¾	POTTERS CHARM (IRE)	6	11-7	(t)	Nigel Twiston-Davies	Sam Twiston-Davies	12/1
6	9½	KAPPA JY PYKE (FR)	5	11-7		W. P. Mullins, Ireland	S. F. O'Keeffe	100/1
7	10	KISS WILL (FR)	5	11-7		W. P. Mullins, Ireland	Mr P. W. Mullins	50/1
8	7	KEL HISTOIRE (FR)	5	11-7		W. P. Mullins, Ireland	M. P. Walsh	33/1
9	25	SIXMILEBRIDGE (IRE)	6	11-7	(t)	Fergal O'Brien	Kielan Woods	16/1
pu		KAID D'AUTHIE (FR)	5	11-7		W. P. Mullins, Ireland	B. Hayes	40/1
pu		SUPERSUNDAE (FR)	6	11-7	(h)	W. P. Mullins, Ireland	D. E. Mullins	50/1

11 ran Race Time 5m 11.10 Closing Sectional (4.10f): 59.0s (102.9%) Winning Owner: Mr John P. McManus

A trio of unbeaten hurdlers at the head of the market made for a fascinating renewal of the Baring Bingham, run under the name of a third sponsor in the last 3 years, and the trio all gave their running, in line at the last, The New Lion the strongest on the run-in, giving British stables a first win in the race since Willoughby Court in 2017; the form looks well up to standard and all 3 are likely to make their mark in open company next season; incidentally, the field was the largest for the race since 2020, Willie Mullins' yard accounting for more than half of those to line up. **The New Lion** who'd changed hands since his win in the Challow, showed significant further improvement in defeating the pick of the Irish in gutsy fashion, likely that he has still more to offer, prices offered for the Champion Hurdle by bookmakers afterwards, and while his pedigree suggests going up in trip rather than down will suit, the way he travels would have you believing a well-run 2m wouldn't pose him too many problems; held up, headway after 3 out, shaken up home turn, hung left, switched approaching last, every chance there, stayed on to lead final 50 yds. **The Yellow Clay** strong in the betting, wasn't quite able to maintain his unbeaten record, though he showed further improvement, a good prospect for the best races next season, whether he stays over hurdles or goes chasing; went prominent after second, led on bridle 2 out, shaken up soon after, headed early in straight, wandered, led again last, hung right run-in, headed final 50 yds. **Final Demand** so impressive at Leopardstown on just his second start over hurdles, was less experienced than the pair that beat him and that was perhaps the main factor in his defeat; he still shaped with plenty of promise, the most imposing of the 3 principals, very much a novice chaser to note for next season, though presumably Punchestown will be on the agenda first, likely to be a major player in whatever he contests there; waited with, took keen hold, not fluent first, headway when not fluent 3 out, shaken up straight, led approaching last, hung left, headed when not fluent there, no extra final 100 yds. **Forty Coats** yet to win a race over hurdles, seemed to excel himself in this much higher grade, even if there was an element of picking up the pieces, running past horses that had been more involved in the race; waited with, lost place seventh, left behind next, rallied entering straight, took fourth final 1f, never on terms. **Potters Charm** in first-time tongue strap (which suggests another explanation for his performance last time), was essentially not good enough, unable to go with the principals in the straight, a useful novice over hurdles and enough about him to think he'll reach a similar level over fences next season; tracked pace, not always fluent, pressed leader seventh, went on 3 out, shaken up next, headed, weakened entering straight, lost fourth final 1f. **Kappa Jy Pyke** had clearly looked promising on his first 2 starts over hurdles and was likely to benefit from the step up in trip, but he was unable to find improvement in this much tougher grade, another who seemed to find the preliminaries a bit much, betraying inexperience; waited with, close up when not fluent 2 out, ridden after, soon done with. **Kiss Will** failed to progress from his hurdling debut, a run that had come off a lengthy absence, perhaps just lacking the experience for a race of this nature for all he looked rather outclassed in the paddock; held up, not fluent fourth, shaken up after seventh, weakened before next; he should stay beyond 2m and could well make progress back in calmer waters. **Kel Histoire** had plenty to find at this level, stepping up markedly in trip (should stay beyond 2m), and he finished well held, looking to lack the maturity required, very much on his toes beforehand; held up, not settle fully, labouring before seventh. **Sixmilebridge** had form that wasn't far behind the pick of these and looked open to improvement, but he ran poorly, the occasion getting to him, on his toes in the paddock and getting very excitable at the start; led, not always fluent, raced freely, joined seventh, weakened before 2 out; clearly his demeanour will need watching, but he is likely to be most effective as a chaser and should do well at that discipline next season. **Kaid d'Authie** had a lot to find in this company and wasn't up to the task, on the back foot very early; held up, mistake first, badly hampered, weakened quickly seventh, pulled up straight; his physique suggests a future over fences. **Supersundae** with just the hood this time, fared no better than he had behind Wingman at Leopardstown, even if he did face a stiff task (no match for the runner-up at Naas the time before); handy, shaken up 3 out, weakened 2 out, pulled up approaching last.

TIMEFORM'S VIEW

Brown Advisory Novices' Chase (Broadway) (Grade 1) (1)

Pos	Btn	Horse	Age	Wgt	Eq	Trainer	Jockey	SP
1		LECKY WATSON (IRE)	7	11-7		W. P. Mullins, Ireland	S. F. O'Keeffe	20/1
2	4	STELLAR STORY (IRE)	8	11-7	(s)	Gordon Elliott, Ireland	Danny Gilligan	22/1
3	hd	BETTER DAYS AHEAD (IRE)	7	11-7	(t)	Gordon Elliott, Ireland	J. W. Kennedy	13/2
4	4¼	GORGEOUS TOM (IRE)	7	11-7		Henry de Bromhead, Ireland	D. J. O'Keeffe	11/1
5	sh	BALLYBURN (IRE)	7	11-7		W. P. Mullins, Ireland	P. Townend	4/7f
6	19	DANCING CITY (FR)	8	11-7		W. P. Mullins, Ireland	D. E. Mullins	8/1
ur		QUAI DE BOURBON (FR)	6	11-7		W. P. Mullins, Ireland	Mr P. W. Mullins	14/1

7 ran Race Time 6m 30.30 Closing Sectional (3.75f): 56s (106.7%) Winning Owner: Slaneyville Syndicate

The week had started rather better than perhaps expected for Britain, with the cards on a chaotic first day largely falling the way of the home team and the big hope in the novice hurdle ranks outgunning a couple of Grade 1 performers from Ireland in the opening Baring Bingham this afternoon, though the picture in the staying chase division must be a good couple of seasons at least from improving, with the Cheltenham Gold Cup declarations featuring only 3 from these shores and this traditional proving ground for the top stayers of the future summoning an even bleaker outlook as it failed to muster even one in a 7-strong field in which only a trio of trainers were represented, the strength-in-numbers approach of Mullins again paying dividends as the biggest price of his group made up for big-gun Ballyburn misfiring at the chief expense of the only runner with a bigger SP all in. **Lecky Watson** remains an inferior force and indeed prospect to stablemate Ballyburn but, unlike that rival, was in the right form and crucially frame of mind in joining that one as well as the second/third in the ranks of winners at the Cheltenham Festival, doing everything right settled in touch in a falsely-run race and not coming back after showing the best turn of pace trying 3m for the first time over fences to burst clear entering the straight, the favourite and the other 2 better-backed stablemates long since out of the picture by the time he began to edge right and idle on the run-in; shortcomings at graded level over hurdles have become a distant memory but whether he's good enough—or indeed has the required stamina—to prove a prolific fixture at the top table over this sort of trip in open company is open to doubt. **Stellar Story** just about outdid his shorter-priced stablemate behind a fellow outsider also overshadowing better-fancied ones from within his own yard, and he'd have done so by a clearer margin—and given the winner something to think about—had this been anything like a true test at this trip, caught out as the gallop lifted soon after 3 out but rallying all the while and edging out old foe Better Days Ahead close to the finish, cut from the cloth of National Hunt Chase types of old but rated too high to get into the facelifted version; his last 2 starts suggest his jumping is getting there all the while. **Better Days Ahead** showed form at least as good in defeat as when clinging on to land the odds against Stellar Story at Navan, on the wrong side of a head-to-head with that rival this time but at level weights instead of in receipt of 5 lb; chased leader, led briefly 3 out, left behind by winner entering straight, kept on, lost second dying strides; he, too, promises to prove more of a top-flight handicapper next season than bona fide Grade 1 stayer. **Gorgeous Tom** ran about as well as could be expected in a more prestigious Grade 1 novice, the longer trip proving within range; in touch, awkward fourth, ridden from 3 out, left behind gradually straight. **Ballyburn** gave negative signals beforehand and some more severe ones in the race itself as he fluffed his lines badly bidding to make it back-to-back odds-on successes in seemingly uncompetitive Grade 1 novices at this meeting, ridden with restraint upped to 3m and not benefiting from it, refusing to settle and launching himself at the seventh, which led to a significant error that shuffled him back to last, a position he improved upon only as stablemate Dancing City wilted in the straight; his win in the Scalp had suggested 3m ought not be a problem and allowing him his head the next time he tries it is surely the way to go. **Dancing City** was uneasy in the betting and produced an atypical finishing effort as he had his winning run ended, having led until a mistake 3 out that looked worse than it probably was (rider unbalanced after steadying him into it seeking a stride). **Quai de Bourbon** overcame a peck at the fifth that saw him drop to the back but not an error at the fourth last, unseating an amateur still chasing a first Grade 1 success over obstacles at this meeting.

Betmgm Queen Mother Champion Chase (Grade 1) (1)

Pos	Btn	Horse	Age	Wgt	Eq	Trainer	Jockey	SP
1		MARINE NATIONALE (IRE)	8	11-10	(t)	Barry Connell, Ireland	Sean Flanagan	5/1
2	18	JONBON (FR)	9	11-10		Nicky Henderson	Nico de Boinville	5/6f
3	1¼	CAPTAIN GUINNESS (IRE)	10	11-10		Henry de Bromhead, Ireland	Rachael Blackmore	25/1
4	½	SOLNESS (FR)	7	11-10	(s+t)	Joseph Patrick O'Brien, Ireland	J. J. Slevin	12/1
5	5½	FOUND A FIFTY (IRE)	8	11-10		Gordon Elliott, Ireland	Danny Gilligan	11/1
F		LIBBERTY HUNTER	9	11-10		Evan Williams	Adam Wedge	33/1
F		QUILIXIOS	8	11-10		Henry de Bromhead, Ireland	D. J. O'Keeffe	40/1
pu		ENERGUMENE (FR)	11	11-10		W. P. Mullins, Ireland	P. Townend	6/1

8 ran Race Time 3m 59.00 Closing Sectional (3.75f): 56.8s (99.2%) Winning Owner: Mr Barry Connell

A Champion Chase that revolved around Jonbon, his form this season well in advance of that shown by the pick of his rivals, the Irish-trained runners among his opponents all with form that was much of a muchness; as with the Champion Hurdle the previous day, the race didn't go to script, Jonbon done no favours by the standing start and his jolting mistake at the ninth enough to effectively end his chance, the race between Marine Nationale and Quilixios soon after 3 out, the former set to gain the upper hand when his rival departed at the last, the performance an improved one, but not so good as the winning margin might suggest, Jonbon's best form still well in advance of what Marine Nationale achieved. **Marine Nationale** winner of the 2023 Supreme Novices' Hurdle, had hinted that he might have more to offer in his 2 defeats by Solness at Leopardstown and duly found further improvement to secure a second Festival prize, though the margin of victory doesn't tell the whole story, not least that Quilixios was still with a chance when he fell at the last; held up, travelled well, smooth headway before 3 out, led when left well clear last, in command run-in; still relatively lightly raced for his age, he'll presumably go to Punchestown, likely to hold good claims to gain a second Grade 1 if faced with just the pick of his domestic rivals. **Jonbon** again calmer in the preliminaries than he used to be, had won all 5 starts, 4 of them at Grade 1 level, since being forced to miss last season's Champion Chase, when his stable was under a cloud, and looked to hold outstanding claims, yet like stable-companion Constitution Hill in the Champion Hurdle, his chance was ruined by a rare jumping lapse, which in his case followed a slightly tardy getaway as a result of the standing start; more patiently ridden than usual as a consequence, he then lost his place completely after a bad mistake at the ninth and was allowed plenty of time to recover, plugging on the straight to take a remote second late on. **Captain Guinness** last year's winner, hadn't shown his form in 3 starts this season and, whilst this was a better effort, he was still some way off his best, perhaps time catching up with him; held up, not fluent fourth, effort after 3 out, left second and mistake last, weakened run-in. **Solness** who took the eye beforehand, had won both the Irish Grade 1s at this trip this winter, beating the winner last time, but he couldn't establish a clear lead this time, not helped by the standing start, and ran some way below form; handy, not fluent first, disputed lead fifth, went on soon after, headed seventh, shaken up after, weakened 3 out. **Found A Fifty** runner-up to Gaelic Warrior in the Arkle last season, had a similar chance on his best form (including a defeat of Solness) to the other Irish-trained challengers, but he'd run as if amiss last time and was again some way below his best on his first start since Christmas, something to prove on the back of those runs; waited with, shaken up after 3 out, left behind soon after. **Libberty Hunter** had a bit to find at this level but was far from done with when he took a nasty-looking fall at the third last, the race still taking shape at that stage, having travelled well dropped out. **Quilixios** at the second attempt, confirmed the improvement shown when chasing home Jonbon in the Tingle Creek, set to finish second when he came down, sure to have been further ahead of the third at the line than the 6 lengths he was up at the time; pressed leader, went on after second, joined fifth, settled behind leader soon after, led again approaching 3 out, shaken up entering straight, headed when fell last. **Energumene** bidding for a third win in the race, reportedly lost his action coming down the hill, which explains his rapid retreat, this just the fourth defeat of his illustrious chasing career, whether he has one final hurrah in him at Punchestown remaining to be seen; led until second, led again seventh, headed before 3 out, soon done with, behind when jumped right 2 out and pulled up.

Weatherbys Champion Bumper (Standard Open National Hunt Flat) (Grade 1) (1)

Pos	Btn	Horse	Age	Wgt	Eq	Trainer	Jockey	SP
1		BAMBINO FEVER (IRE)	5	11-0		W. P. Mullins, Ireland	Miss J. Townend	4/1
2	1½	HEADS UP	5	11-7		John McConnell, Ireland	Sean Bowen	33/1
3	1½	SHUTTLE DIPLOMACY (FR)	5	11-7		Thomas Cooper, Ireland	Donagh Meyler	66/1
4	hd	CABALLERO CLIFF	4	10-11		Robert Stephens	Ben Jones	150/1
5	1¾	EL CAIROS (FR)	5	11-7		Gary & Josh Moore	Mr David Maxwell	28/1
6	1½	IDAHO SUN (IRE)	5	11-7		Harry Fry	Bryan Carver	18/1
7	½	SORTUDO (IRE)	5	11-7		W. P. Mullins, Ireland	D. E. Mullins	33/1
8	1¼	HE CAN'T DANCE (IRE)	5	11-7		Gordon Elliott, Ireland	Mr H. C. Swan	33/1
9	¾	NO DRAMA THIS END (IRE)	5	11-7		Paul Nicholls	Harry Cobden	12/1
10	1	COPACABANA	5	11-7		W. P. Mullins, Ireland	Mr P. W. Mullins	9/2
11	hd	KALYPSO'CHANCE (FR)	5	11-7		Gordon Elliott, Ireland	Danny Gilligan	5/2f
12	ns	GAMEOFINCHES	6	11-7		W. P. Mullins, Ireland	P. Townend	6/1
13	¾	I STARTED A JOKE (IRE)	6	11-7		Charles Byrnes, Ireland	P. Byrnes	33/1
14	1¼	FORTUNE DE MER (IRE)	5	11-7		Dan Skelton	Harry Skelton	20/1
15	6½	DALSTON LAD (IRE)	5	11-7		Dan Skelton	Tristan Durrell	66/1
16	nk	LANCELOT ALLEN (FR)	4	10-11		Mrs Jane Williams	David Noonan	200/1
17	65	AQUA FORCE (IRE)	6	11-0		W. P. Mullins, Ireland	M. P. Walsh	11/1

17 ran Race Time 4m 00.30 Closing Sectional (4.10f): 54.7s (109.8%) Winning Owner: O'Connell Morgan Syndicate

Year in, year out, the Champion Bumper brings together a large field of highly promising horses and proves a useful guide to potential for going over hurdles and later fences, this running likely to be no exception, even if this has the look of a rather substandard renewal, none of the field having run to a level close to that usually required beforehand, the field finishing in too much of a heap—off a steadier pace than typical for the race—to take a high view of the form; Willie Mullins sent out just the 5 runners, but they included the winner, his fourteenth success in the race and fifth in the last 6 years, though his next runner home could manage only seventh and this wasn't the total whitewash for British stables that it sometimes is, the fourth, fifth and sixth all representing the home team, the fifth not having much luck in running. **Bambino Fever** well supported against male rivals, maintained her unbeaten record with a smart effort, by no means the pick of these on looks but clearly with plenty of potential for hurdling next season, her amateur rider seen to good effect, steering a wide course into the straight but out of trouble, unlike several of those to chase her home who took a much tighter route; waited with, took keen hold, headway 4f out, shaken up entering straight, stayed on to lead well inside final 1f. **Heads Up** the most exposed/experienced in the field, showed much improved form after 3 months off, very much seen to advantage the way things unfolded; led, shaken up 3f out, headed well inside final 1f; he still has some filling out to do. **Shuttle Diplomacy** last seen when down the field in the Grade 1 bumper at Punchestown last spring, looked in good shape and showed much improved form, doing his best work at the finish; held up, took keen hold, effort entering straight, hung right over 1f out, stayed on approaching final 1f, took third close home. **Caballero Cliff** looked an extremely optimistic runner at this level and excelled himself, emerging best of the British-trained runners, and that despite not having the best of runs through; in touch, headway early final circuit, short of room home turn, shaken up straight, kept on, lost third close home. **El Cairos** after 4 months off, was much improved from bumper debut, shaping even better than the bare result suggests after having a rough passage from the turn, all in all plenty to like about his effort; held up, smooth headway approaching straight, pushed along 2f out, bumped over 1f out, hung left, one paced inside final 1f. **Idaho Sun** progressed again, despite not looking ideally served by the way the race unfolded, doing his best work at the finish, not at all a bad type and having the makings of a useful staying novice hurdler next season; mid-division, lost place over 3f out, rallied over 1f out, kept on well. **Sortudo** ran well upped in grade, second home of his stable's quintet, though he was well positioned when the tempo increased and had plenty of experience compared to some; mid-division, tracked pace 4f out, shaken up under 3f out, one paced straight. **He Can't Dance** by the same sire as the winner, though a rather better type, progressed again, though better placed than most and given quite a hard race too; close up, shaken up over 3f out, driven straight, one paced. **No Drama This End** an athletic sort, acquitted himself pretty well on the back of just one run, improving on that debut effort after 10 weeks off, more of a stayer than ideal for the way this developed; in touch, took keen hold, tracked pace 4f out, shaken up over 2f out, one paced. **Copacabana** has plenty about him physically but he looked short on experience and ran to just a similar level as on debut, still a useful prospect with hurdling in mind next season; held up, headway 4f out, shaken up approaching straight, outpaced soon after. **Kalypso'chance** had looked an exciting prospect in winning his first 2 starts, but he came up short in this much tougher contest after 3 months off, lacking a change of pace; prominent, travelled well, every chance approaching straight, shaken up home turn, one paced. **Gameofinches** about the pick of the field on looks and with plenty to like about his pedigree and debut win, ran only to a similar level as he had then, though shaped better than the result, likely in need of the experience more than most and to have benefited from a stronger gallop; held up, not settle fully, smooth headway over 3f out, shaken up entering straight, ran green, weakened late on; he's finished in the second half of the field but is a better prospect than quite a few that beat him. **I Started A Joke** one of the better types in the paddock and likely to have a future over hurdles, had shown himself a useful prospect in 2 starts in Ireland without suggesting he was up to this grade; held up, headway 4f out, shaken up entering straight, lost place soon after. **Fortune de Mer** faced a very stiff task in this company and beat only a few home having been very much on his toes beforehand; in rear, some headway 4f out, shaken up entering straight, weakened soon after. **Dalston Lad** had won both his starts in bumpers, but in small fields, and, sent off at long odds, made no impact in this much tougher race; waited with, shaken up 4f out, lost place soon after. **Lancelot Allen** off 3 months and one of just 2 4-y-os in the field, faced a very stiff task in this grade; held up, shaken up over 3f out, labouring soon after; he has scope and a decent pedigree, so may well have a future over hurdles. **Aqua Force** had switched stables since her winning debut on heavy ground, but this presumably came too soon for she ran no sort of race, in trouble soon after halfway and tailed off 3f out.

CHELTENHAM Thursday March 13
GOOD TO SOFT

Ryanair Mares' Novices' Hurdle (Dawn Run) (Grade 2)

Pos	Btn	Horse	Age	Wgt	Eq	Trainer	Jockey	SP
1		AIR OF ENTITLEMENT (IRE)	6	11-4		Henry de Bromhead, Ireland	Rachael Blackmore	16/1
2	½	SIXANDAHALF (IRE)	5	11-4		Gavin Patrick Cromwell, Ireland	Keith Donoghue	85/40f
3	6	DIVA LUNA (IRE)	6	11-4		Ben Pauling	Ben Jones	12/1
4	2½	KAROLINE BANBOU (FR)	5	11-4		W. P. Mullins, Ireland	M. P. Walsh	10/1
5	2¼	METKAYINA (IRE)	6	11-4		Noel Williams	Jonathan Burke	50/1
6	nk	GALILEO DAME (IRE)	4	10-8		Joseph Patrick O'Brien, Ireland	J. J. Slevin	9/2
7	2	KARAMOJA (FR)	5	11-4	(h)	W. P. Mullins, Ireland	J. W. Kennedy	28/1
8	5½	JUBILEE ALPHA (IRE)	6	11-4		Paul Nicholls	Harry Cobden	15/2
9	nk	TOUR OVALIE (FR)	6	11-4		Evan Williams	Isabel Williams	100/1
10	½	JANE EIRE (IRE)	5	11-4	(h+t)	Henry de Bromhead, Ireland	Sean Bowen	66/1
11	2	AURORA VEGA (IRE)	7	11-4		W. P. Mullins, Ireland	P. Townend	9/1
12	¾	MAGIC MCCOLGAN (IRE)	6	11-4		W. P. Mullins, Ireland	D. E. Mullins	100/1
13	2	KITTY FOYLE (IRE)	5	11-4		Daisy Hitchins	Harry Reed	200/1
14	2	KIMI DE MAI (FR)	5	11-4	(h+t)	W. P. Mullins, Ireland	S. F. O'Keeffe	66/1
15	nk	QUEENIE ST CLAIR (IRE)	5	11-4		E. Sheehy, Ireland	Sean Flanagan	250/1
16	¾	VENUSIENNE (FR)	5	11-4		W. P. Mullins, Ireland	B. Hayes	33/1
17	2¼	MYSTICAL GODDESS (IRE)	6	11-4	(t)	Henry de Bromhead, Ireland	D. J. O'Keeffe	150/1
18	12	BRENDAS ASKING (IRE)	7	11-4		Kim Bailey & Mat Nicholls	Tom Bellamy	200/1
19	1¼	LAGERTHA (FR)	5	11-4		Katy Price	S. Fitzgerald	200/1
20	18	MAUGHREEN (IRE)	6	11-4	(h)	W. P. Mullins, Ireland	Mr P. W. Mullins	11/1
pu		BLUEY (IRE)	6	11-4		Emma Lavelle	Harry Skelton	14/1
pu		HOLLYGROVE CHA CHA (IRE)	5	11-4		Jamie Snowden	Gavin Sheehan	22/1
pu		JUST A ROSE (FR)	6	11-4		Paul Nicholls	Freddie Gingell	25/1

23 ran   Race Time 4m 04.50   Closing Sectional (3.80f): 53.5s (103.3%)   Winning Owner: Robcour

The biggest ever field for the Dawn Run and a competitive race even if plenty looked outmatched physically and were making up the numbers, the form between the first 2 well up to the useful standard typically required, a strong finish from the winner seeing her catch the strong-travelling favourite in the final strides; the pace was good and it was a fair race once underway, though yet another shambolic standing start after a failed first try—Maughreen in particular had her race ruined—underlined that the starting procedures require urgent review. **Air of Entitlement** defied the drop in trip to land a big prize on just her second outing over hurdles, not travelling nearly as well as the runner-up but powering up the hill to get up late on; mid-division, shaken up on inner home turn, good progress on inner early in straight, challenged after last, found plenty to lead near finish; she can surely only be better back over further and that bodes extremely well for her finding further improvement and winning more good races, including over fences when the time comes. **Sixandahalf** succumbed to a stronger stayer late on but only having powered through the race in the style of a mare of rare quality, looking the pick of them for nearly the whole way; close up, travelled powerfully, produced to lead before last, tackled flat, collared dying strides, clear of rest; she hasn't reached her limit yet and there should be plenty of good races in her over the coming seasons, on the Flat as well as over jumps. **Diva Luna** ran a fine race in faring best of the British, in the firing line throughout and held only after the last; chased leaders, typically jumped well, led 2 out, headed approaching last, jumped left there, one paced; she's got the style and demeanour of an even better chaser. **Karoline Banbou** ran well in doing best of the Mullins 7; in touch, travelled well, went third home turn, no extra before last; she may well do better again, still only 3 starts into her time with her masterful trainer after all. **Metkayina** improved in the face of a stiffish task, doing well considering she was one of those inconvenienced at the start; slowly into stride, held up, ridden 2 out, kept on well flat; her dam won over as far as 2¾m and she's ready for a return to further herself (will be suited by 2½m). **Galileo Dame** the only juvenile in the field running here instead of in the Triumph, seemed to get a little lost in a well-run, big-field race but did enough to think she's value for the useful form she showed at Leopardstown; mid-division, off pace third, ridden 2 out, rallied last, kept on; she may well benefit from this experience and will have no trouble staying 2½m. **Karamoja** acquitted herself well considering she had plenty to find on form; chased leaders, effort between last 2, not fluent last, no extra. **Jubilee Alpha** looked the pick of the British but underperformed, doing a few things wrong on the way round; prominent, not settle fully, mistake 3 out, effort soon after next, weakened last. **Tour Ovalie** predictably wasn't good enough but showed she's still in top form by briefly getting competitive, her performance encouraging for her prospects of resuming her progress back in the right grade; held up, headway after 3 out, in touch home turn, left behind before last. **Jane Eire** wasn't discredited considering the stiffness of the task after 4 months off; raced wide, raced well off the pace, ridden 2 out, late headway but never in it; she wears a hood but has stamina in her pedigree to think at least 2½m should suit. **Aurora Vega** was below form, probably more to it than the drop in trip not suiting; raced wide, effort home turn, weakened before last. **Magic McColgan** ran about as well as at Punchestown without being up to the task; mid-division, off pace third, ridden after 2 out, made no impression; her bumper form was fairly useful and she may yet reach that level as a hurdler with her sights lowered. **Kitty Foyle** last seen on the Flat, was out of depth; held up, bad mistake 2 out, made no impression. **Kimi de Mai** faced too stiff a task; held up, ridden after 2 out, weakened before last; she may yet progress with her sights lowered. **Queenie St Clair** was way out of her depth; always behind. **Venusienne** a fairly useful second on her only start in France, found this too tough an ask on first outing since leaving P. & C. Peltier after 18 months off but showed up well to a point and remains capable of better for her outstanding new stable; mid-field, ridden home turn, weakened before last. **Mystical Goddess** was well held, not up to the company over an inadequate trip; held up, made no impression. **Brendas Asking** probably remains in form, paying in the end for forcing the pace; led until 2 out, weakened. **Lagertha** wasn't up to this better company; slowly into stride, held up, ridden

2 out, made no impression. **Maughreen** in a hood, can have a line put through this run, done for by the standing start; whipped round start and very slowly away, soon detached. **Bluey** ran poorly; mid-division, in touch third, weakened before 2 out. **Hollygrove Cha Cha** ran the first stinker of her career, struggling with a well-run 2m but probably beaten by more than just that; mid-division, well beaten after 3 out. **Just A Rose** found this a total shock to the system, not coping at all with the demanding test; mid-division, mistakes second, 4 out, weakened after 3 out.

Ryanair Chase (Festival Trophy) (Grade 1) (1)

Pos	Btn	Horse	Age	Wgt	Eq	Trainer	Jockey	SP
1		FACT TO FILE (FR)	8	11-10		W. P. Mullins, Ireland	M. P. Walsh	6/4f
2	9	HEART WOOD (FR)	7	11-10		Henry de Bromhead, Ireland	D. J. O'Keeffe	18/1
3	8½	ENVOI ALLEN (FR)	11	11-10	(t)	Henry de Bromhead, Ireland	Rachael Blackmore	12/1
4	2¼	PROTEKTORAT (FR)	10	11-10	(t)	Dan Skelton	Harry Skelton	5/1
5	2½	MASTER CHEWY (IRE)	8	11-10		Nigel Twiston-Davies	Sam Twiston-Davies	40/1
6	3¾	IL EST FRANCAIS (FR)	7	11-10		N. George & A. Zetterholm, France	James Reveley	10/3
7	39	DJELO (FR)	7	11-10		Venetia Williams	Charlie Deutsch	15/2
pu		HANG IN THERE (IRE)	11	11-10		Emma Lavelle	Harry Cobden	66/1
pu		JUNGLE BOOGIE (IRE)	11	11-10		Henry de Bromhead, Ireland	D. E. Mullins	16/1

9 ran Race Time 5m 10.20 Closing Sectional (3.84f): 56.70s (102.1%) Winning Owner: Mr John P. McManus

A race still often viewed as an inferior to the Championship races at 2m and 3¼m but one with a habit of eclipsing its revered counterparts, which may well prove the case again with only the Gold Cup standing in the way of the contrary, as Fact To File did what stablemates Allaho, Un de Sceaux and Vautour had done before him in this in the past decade by delivering a complete display that merited being rated right up there with the best performances of the season, the winners from the lesser editions of 2023 and 2024 forced to settle for a remote third and fourth respectively. **Fact To File** produced a first-rate—indeed flawless—performance to justify connections' decision to drop back for the Ryanair having spent the bulk of the season on the standard trail for a Broadway winner heading towards the Cheltenham Gold Cup, making dismantling a Grade 1 field seem remarkably unremarkable as he jumped and travelled superbly stalking a pace not so scorching as expected and then didn't look back after jumping past his apparently main adversary 3 out, so dominant that he was able to be eased late on; another crack at Galopin des Champs will surely follow down the line, maybe even as soon as Punchestown (where Fact To File lowered his colours in the John Durkan), though in terms of next season the rematch may be best kept until the Gold Cup, with a first half of the campaign aimed at a King George making more sense than trying to tackle an opponent so formidable around Leopardstown. **Heart Wood** proved he isn't quite in the winner's league whilst showing he is of Grade-1 calibre set against more conventional lines, giving a far clearer account of what he can do in a well-run race back down from 3m; waited with, he made good progress 4 out and stayed on all the while in vain pursuit after taking second approaching 2 out, pulling clear of the last 2 winners of this race in the process; he looks an ideal type for the Melling at Aintree if allowed to take his chance so soon (gap only 3 weeks this year). **Envoi Allen** maintained his record of having never finished worse than third when completing across a 7-year span of Festival appearances (first, second and third in this last 3 seasons) that has shone a light on both his consistency and durability, not at quite the same level as at times in the past but near to finishing about as close as he could up against an outstanding winner and a runner-up only recently on the Grade 1 scene, pushed along in fifth before the straight yet keeping at it well enough to have claimed third by the last. **Protektorat** wasn't nearly the same force as he'd been on testing ground in this last year, unable to uphold positions with Envoi Allen never mind retain his crown, which would have been beyond him even at his best anyway given how much higher a level Fact To File hit in comparison with the 2024 renewal; tracked pace, shaken up before 3 out, not quicken. **Master Chewy** came up short for ability more than stamina trying this trip for the first time over fences, though there will be other softer graded openings on these shores for him to again pay his way next season; held up, headway under pressure approaching straight, no further impression. **Il Est Francais** has dazzled on his last 2 visits to Britain but merely gave the latest of so many examples down the years of how potency around Kempton in a King George is no free pass to a successful transition to Cheltenham, not ridden quite so forcefully as might have been expected dropping in trip (didn't lead until jumping on seventh) yet still having nothing left once headed 3 out, losing a further 4 positions in the straight; he'll give Fact To File a bigger scare if they were to meet at Kempton. **Djelo** didn't fire at all for a yard with only one odds-on winner to show for the last 4 weeks or so, his Turners third at the 2024 Festival suggesting the track wasn't sufficient excuse; raced off the pace, lost ground fourth, never going well after, laboured headway 3 out, no further impression, eased off. **Hang In There** has never won later in a season than November (when the competition rises) and was way out of his depth in any case after 4 months off; soon behind, mistake eighth, lost touch. **Jungle Boogie** is better than this but, at this level, found what had started as bold jumping begin to crack once headed, having been a rather surprise leader until the seventh, losing second soon after belting the eleventh before dropping away quickly.

Paddy Power Stayers' Hurdle (Grade 1) (1)

Pos	Btn	Horse	Age	Wgt	Eq	Trainer	Jockey	SP
1		BOB OLINGER (IRE)	10	11-10		Henry de Bromhead, Ireland	Rachael Blackmore	8/1
2	1¾	TEAHUPOO (FR)	8	11-10		Gordon Elliott, Ireland	J. W. Kennedy	7/4f
3	8	THE WALLPARK (IRE)	7	11-10		Gordon Elliott, Ireland	M. P. Walsh	7/1
4	½	ROCKY'S DIAMOND (IRE)	5	11-10		Declan Queally, Ireland	S. Fitzgerald	28/1
5	1½	BUDDY ONE (IRE)	8	11-10	(t)	Paul John Gilligan, Ireland	Jack G. Gilligan	50/1
6	8½	FRANCISCAN ROCK (IRE)	8	11-10	(s+t)	M. F. Morris, Ireland	Gavin Peter Brouder	80/1
7	6	LUCKY PLACE (FR)	6	11-10		Nicky Henderson	Nico de Boinville	11/2
8	12	GOWEL ROAD (IRE)	9	11-10		Nigel Twiston-Davies	Sam Twiston-Davies	33/1
F		CRAMBO	8	11-10	(t)	Fergal O'Brien	Jonathan Burke	40/1
ur		HOME BY THE LEE (IRE)	10	11-10	(b)	Joseph Patrick O'Brien, Ireland	J. J. Slevin	13/2
pu		GA LAW (FR)	9	11-10	(s)	Jamie Snowden	Gavin Sheehan	50/1
pu		MYSTICAL POWER (IRE)	6	11-10	(h)	W. P. Mullins, Ireland	P. Townend	14/1
pu		NEMEAN LION (GER)	8	11-10		Kerry Lee	Richard Patrick	16/1

13 ran Race Time 5m 59.10 Closing Sectional (3.80f): 53.1s (107.2%) Winning Owner: Robcour

It's a while now since this division has had a real standout—Thistlecrack in 2016 was the last winner of this to show top-class form on the day—and the search for one continues after a Stayers' Hurdle that saw one of the joint-oldest in the field get the better of last year's winner as the pair drew clear approaching the last, the form between them right in line with the more recently established standards; the pace threatened to be strong early after Gowel Road shot into the lead, though it didn't take long for things to steady down and an above-par finishing sectional shows the race became more a test of speed than stamina at the trip. **Bob Olinger** really comes alive at Cheltenham and took his unbeaten record at the track to 4 (including 3

Festival win, one of them admittedly fortunate) with a performance up there with the very best he's produced, his trainer—who with this success along with Racheal Blackmore completed a full house of the Festival's open Grade 1 events—deserving plenty of credit for getting him to this level aged 10 after his career had at one point threatened to go off the rails; settled out the back, he made smooth progress into contention 2 out, was humoured along onto Teahupoo's heels approaching the last (where he typically carried his head a little awkwardly) and quickened decisively ahead early on the flat, seeing out the trip thoroughly in a race that was more a test of finishing speed than it was out-and-out staying power; he's got Aintree (close second in the Aintree Hurdle last year but has the Liverpool Hurdle as a compelling alternative this time) and Punchestown as options for later in the spring. **Teahupoo** arrived following an identical preparation to when winning this last season (albeit having finished second in the Hatton's Grace rather than winning it) and probably ran no worse even though failing to defend his crown, doing pretty much everything right along the way as he made smooth and steady progress to lead early in the straight, unable to match the winner's turn of foot after the last but sticking at it to come clear of the rest; he'll presumably be freshened up for a bid at a repeat success in the Champion Stayers at Punchestown, and softer ground and a more strongly-run race are both factors that could tilt things in his favour should he meet the winner again there; beyond that, he's still young enough to have a few more seasons at this sort of level. **The Wallpark** ran just about his best race yet faced with his toughest task to date, a slightly enigmatic character but with an exemplary record of late; waited with towards the rear, he had to dodge the faller at the sixth, lost his place briefly 4 out but made good headway once switched wide after the next, laying down a strong challenge to stable-companion Teahupoo early in the straight and held only on the run to the last, not unusually carrying his tail a little awkwardly on the run-in; provided he keeps his quirks in check, he's young enough to remain a prominent figure on the staying scene for a few seasons yet. **Rocky's Diamond** underlined all the progress he's made this season with a fine effort; pressed leader, upsides sixth, edged ahead 2 out, headed early in straight, plugged on; he's a youngster in any terms, let alone those of staying hurdlers, and there's no saying he's peaked just yet considering the overall trajectory of his form. **Buddy One** back in a tongue strap, ran well in this race for the second year running and at the Festival for the third, not that he ever looked like doing better; mid-division, lost place before 2 out, rallied last, plugged on. **Franciscan Rock** shaped as if still in good form, if anything better than the result considering he moved into fourth early in the straight; held up, travelled well, headway 2 out, effort before last, weakened flat. **Lucky Place** had his winning run ended, the company and the trip part of the problem (had more to do on form that being second favourite might've suggested), though some scruffy jumping didn't help either; prominent, mistakes second, 4 out, effort 2 out, weakened before last; it's still been a fine season and there should be more good races in him, including if he's given a try over fences. **Gowel Road** just wasn't up to the company; soon led, joined sixth, faded from 2 out. **Crambo** was in touch when taking a crunching fall at the sixth. **Home By The Lee** was left with nowhere to go when Crambo fell in front of him at the sixth; he'd beaten Bob Olinger at Leopardstown and Navan on his last 2 outings, albeit getting weight at the latter and with that one below his best at the former. **Ga Law** faced a stiff task for a rare try hurdling but, concerningly, again looked less than enthusiastic; held up, blundered fourth, reminders after, never going well, well held 3 out. **Mystical Power** who sweated up beforehand, looked an unlikely stayer even in a refitted hood but just ran as if amiss; held up, eased off after 3 out, pulled up before next; it's been a real write-off of a season after such a good novice campaign and he's got plenty to prove. **Nemean Lion** turned in a rare poor effort, probably more to it than the trip even if he is a doubtful stayer; mid-division, weakened after 2 out.

CHELTENHAM Friday March 14
GOOD TO SOFT

Jcb Triumph Hurdle (Grade 1) (1)

Pos	Btn	Horse	Age	Wgt	Eq	Trainer	Jockey	SP
1		PONIROS	4	11-2		W. P. Mullins, Ireland	Jonjo O'Neill Jr.	100/1
2	nk	LULAMBA (FR)	4	11-2		Nicky Henderson	Nico de Boinville	11/4
3	¾	EAST INDIA DOCK	4	11-2		James Owen	Sam Twiston-Davies	5/4f
4	1¾	LADY VEGA ALLEN (FR)	4	10-9		W. P. Mullins, Ireland	P. Townend	14/1
5	1¼	PLACE DE LA NATION (FR)	4	10-9		W. P. Mullins, Ireland	Danny Gilligan	100/1
6	1½	HELLO NEIGHBOUR (IRE)	4	11-2	(h)	Gavin Patrick Cromwell, Ireland	Keith Donoghue	7/2
7	9	TOO BOSSY FOR US (IRE)	4	11-2		W. P. Mullins, Ireland	Harry Cobden	50/1
8	½	SAINTE LUCIE (FR)	4	10-9	(h)	W. P. Mullins, Ireland	D. E. Mullins	50/1
9	15	MONDO MAN	4	11-2	(h)	Gary & Josh Moore	Brian Hughes	33/1
10	7	LUMIERE DU LARGE (FR)	4	10-9	(t)	W. P. Mullins, Ireland	K. C. Sexton	200/1
11	1¼	WILLY DE HOUELLE (FR)	4	11-2	(h+t)	W. P. Mullins, Ireland	B. Hayes	40/1
12	14	CHARLUS (IRE)	4	11-2		W. P. Mullins, Ireland	S. F. O'Keeffe	66/1
13	3¾	LARZAC (FR)	4	11-2	(t)	W. P. Mullins, Ireland	M. P. Walsh	33/1
pu		OPEC	4	10-9		James Owen	Sean Bowen	150/1
pu		BLUE LEMONS (IRE)	4	11-2		W. P. Mullins, Ireland	Rachael Blackmore	12/1
pu		GIBBS ISLAND	4	11-2		Tom Lacey	Stan Sheppard	28/1
pu		PAPPANO	4	11-2		W. P. Mullins, Ireland	Sean Flanagan	150/1

17 ran   Race Time 4m 02.40   Closing Sectional (3.80f): 52.9s (103.6%)   Winning Owner: Tony Bloom

Willie Mullins saddled an absurd eleven of the seventeen runners, 7 of whom were having their first start for the stable, with 3 of that number hurdling debutants, all adding up to a rather punter-unfriendly mix; nevertheless, this bucked the trend of recent years in that the top 2 in the betting were British-trained, and both East India Dock and Lulamba ran fine races to hold every chance after the last only to succumb to one of those Mullins newcomers, 100/1 shot Poniros becoming the longest-priced winner in the race's history in coming from off the pace to get up near the finish; the gallop was brisk and the winner was perhaps helped by others having taken each other on from some way out, but it's not as if it was a total pace collapse and he looks good value for an up-to-scratch winning performance. **Poniros** a useful middle-distance handicapper on the Flat for Ralph Beckett (winless on the Flat in 2024 but with some strong form and sold for 200,000 gns), caused the biggest shock in the history of the Triumph Hurdle on his first outing over timber, a remarkable effort to overcome his inexperience and show smart form right away even if he may have benefited from the market leaders taking each other on from some way out; understandably given time to find his stride, he made good headway into contention 2 out, was clearly still closing on the run to the last and found plenty on the run-in to get ahead near the finish; there's no reason why he shouldn't progress, and one or both of Aintree and Punchestown will give him the opportunity to prove this was no one-off. **Lulamba** might have lost his unbeaten record but in every other respect enhanced an already lofty reputation and looks the best long-term prospect in this field, not least as he's a jumps bred who was one of the standouts in the paddock, looking in extremely good shape; travelling fluently up with the pace, he started to challenge when untidy 2 out and battled on well up the run-in to edge out East India Dock only to find the winner finishing even more strongly on the other side of that rival; either Aintree or Punchestown will provide him with excellent opportunities to win a Grade 1 later this spring, and he's a really exciting prospect for next season whether kept to hurdles or sent chasing. **East India Dock** matched his form from Trials day here rather than finding any more progress as he had his winning run ended, no excuses needed even if his jumping was a little more mixed than it had been that day, still electric at times but scruffy on other occasions; he raced up with the pace, hitting 4 out and doing the same when upsides 2 out, still managing to go about a length up approaching the last before being worn down by 2 stronger finishers on the run to the line; the margins here were sufficiently fine to give connections plenty of optimism that he could reverse form with the first 2 should they meet again in the spring and there should be plenty more good races in him over the coming seasons, back on the Flat as well as over jumps. **Lady Vega Allen** ran well as she fared best of the ones that had raced in Ireland, going rather keenly but seeing it out well; raced wide, prominent, went with zest, led third, joined when not fluent 2 out, not quicken before last, stayed on flat; a sturdy filly, she's bred for jumping (from the family of Quevega) and will stay 2½m **Place de La Nation** showed much improved form at huge odds, looking well at home at this level; in touch, challenged after 2 out, not quicken before last, kept on; connections will presumably be keen to preserve her novice status and it's easy to see her back at this meeting next year as a leading contender for the Dawn Run, though she'll stay 2½m if required. **Hello Neighbour** ran creditably but lost his unbeaten record as he failed to confirm superiority over the third, a late mistake and the uphill run to the line finding him out; in touch, effort early in straight, mistake last, no extra; he's made rapid strides in just 5 outings Flat and jumps since September, so it would be no surprise if there's still some progress in him **Too Bossy For Us** useful on the Flat for Kevin Philippart de Foy (sold 330,000 gns), couldn't match the remarkable exploits of his winning stable companion but still reached a high level for a newcomer and is sure to benefit from the educational ride he received; dropped out, shaken up 2 out, kept on gradually, never on terms; connections may well be keen to keep him a novice but there's no doubt he'll be winning races over hurdles sooner rather than later, with progress on the cards. **Sainte Lucie** ran a lot better than last time with a hood added without building on the positive impression she'd created at Punchestown at the end of December; raced wide, held up, in touch after 3 out, weakened before last. **Mondo Man** ran below his form from the Adonis, more settled than he had been then in a hood for the first time but not up to this level, also making the worst mistake of the whole race early on; mid-division, flattened second, shaken up after 2 out, made no impression; on the plus side, he'll still be a novice next season and will surely win races, the nature of good handicaps at this sort of trip likely to suit him ideally (already has a fair-looking BHA mark of 124). **Lumiere du Large** a Flat winner in France for E. Grall who'd finished second on her hurdling debut there, raced freely minus the hood worn then and just found this more than she could handle; off pace, took strong hold, beaten after 2 out; she's joined a peerless trainer and may yet progress at the right level. **Willy de Houelle** had the form to run a lot better than he did but flopped; held up, ridden 2 out, made no impression. **Charlus** wasn't up to this better company but may yet progress at a more appropriate level; mid-division, off pace 4 out, no threat after. **Larzac** a fairly useful second on his only outing in France for J. Boisnard, didn't get competitive at all faced with a stiff task after 5 months off; in rear, ridden 2 out, soon beaten; a well-made gelding, he was one of the picks of the paddock along with the runner-up and that's reason enough to give him another chance to progress. **Opec** was out of her depth but seems to have lost her form anyway considering how quickly she lost the lead; raced freely, led until third, weakening when mistake next. **Blue Lemons** went off the shortest of her trainer's 11 but didn't cope with the rise in grade; mid-division, lost place before 2 out. **Gibbs Island** raced too freely to give himself any chance of figuring; in touch, took strong hold, weakened before 2 out; good 2m handicaps should be his arena next season. **Pappano** had Flat form (for the Gosdens, sold 200,000 gns) at least as good as his fellow hurdling newcomers the winner and seventh but just looked badly in need of the experience thrown in at the deep end; novicey mistakes, always behind; he should do better with his sights lowered.

Mrs Paddy Power Mares' Chase (Liberthine) (Grade 2) (1)

Pos	Btn	Horse	Age	Wgt	Eq	Trainer	Jockey	SP
1		DINOBLUE (FR)	8	11-7	(t)	W. P. Mullins, Ireland	M. P. Walsh	6/4f
2	8½	BRIDES HILL (IRE)	8	11-5		Gavin Patrick Cromwell, Ireland	Keith Donoghue	9/2
3	5½	SHECOULDBEANYTHING (IRE)	8	11-2	(t)	Gordon Elliott, Ireland	Danny Gilligan	12/1
4	5	MAYHEM MYA	8	11-2		Chris Honour	Bryan Carver	50/1
5	13	LIMERICK LACE (IRE)	8	11-5	(s)	Gavin Patrick Cromwell, Ireland	J. W. Kennedy	7/2
6	15	ROYALE MARGAUX (FR)	7	11-2	(t)	Tom Symonds	Ben Poste	28/1
7	21	FONTAINE COLLONGES (FR)	10	11-2	(b)	Venetia Williams	Charlie Deutsch	66/1
8	9½	JE T'AI PORTE (IRE)	7	11-2	(h)	Gavin Patrick Cromwell, Ireland	S. Fitzgerald	100/1
F		ALLEGORIE DE VASSY (FR)	8	11-2	(t)	W. P. Mullins, Ireland	P. Townend	4/1

9 ran   Race Time 5m 07.10   Closing Sectional (3.84f): 54.9s (104.4%)   Winning Owner: Mr John P. McManus

The most progressive chasing mare on these shores—Telepathique—wasn't declared but the continued Irish domination by the same couple of yards is by no means the only factor if it's one at all in a continuing feeling that this is a recent addition to the Festival that hasn't hit the ground running, with this year's field a blend of the same old faces and ambitious entrants, none of whom—unlike the odd few in its mares equivalents over hurdles—have realistic hopes of developing into major players in open company. **Dinoblue** made amends for her defeat at the hands of Limerick Lace—not to mention her 2 preceding Festival reverses—ridden with more purpose than on more testing ground in the 2024 renewal, doing everything right (jumped/travelled fluently) close up and already taking the measure of old rival and stablemate Allegorie de Vassy in a 3-length lead when that one's final act in a wayward jumping display left her well clear; she's met with defeat on her last 4 tries outside mares company, however. **Brides Hill** suffered the same fate she had when up against the best of the British crop (absent Telepathique) at Huntingdon, except in this case she'd have been a place worse without Allegorie de Vassy's fall ahead, no excuses on the day; in touch, third when pushed along approaching straight, held when left second last, no match for winner. **Shecouldbeanything** is proving as reliable as ever, doing all she could at this level after 11 weeks off, the bigger fences not posing a problem despite her lack of stature; in touch, outpaced after 3 out, rallied briefly but held when left in a place last. **Mayhem Mya** seemed to excel herself back chasing but, in truth, was never a factor after finding herself outpaced after 5 out. **Limerick Lace** proved all the more disappointing considering she'd won this race (on more testing ground, admittedly) at the chief expense of Dinoblue in 2024, first-time cheekpieces and a 10-week rest not halting her slide, even with the market speaking for her late; waited with, outpaced soon after 3 out, no response straight. **Royale Margaux** faced a stiff task in this grade back chasing but went on the bridle for long enough to deduce she's still in good heart; held up, shaken up after 3 out, no response. **Fontaine Collonges** made no appeal on paper for a test like this (best at 3m+ on bottomless ground), first-time blinkers making no odds on the day; in touch early but soon uncomfortable with pace and lost ground before halfway, labouring some way out. **Je T'ai Porte** might as well have not turned up, normally a front runner but setting off last after missing the break returning from 6 months off and tailed off before 3 out. **Allegorie de Vassy** was in the process of finishing behind superior stablemate Dinoblue again when her race ended slightly prematurely, that she fell at the last no great surprise given she'd already fired a few warning shots by jumping right pretty much throughout as she made the running, set to be put in her place to the tune of more like 5 lengths this time, 3 lengths down when she departed having been claimed at the second last.

Albert Bartlett Novices' Hurdle (Spa) (Grade 1) (1)

Pos	Btn	Horse	Age	Wgt	Eq	Trainer	Jockey	SP
1		JASMIN DE VAUX (FR)	6	11-7		W. P. Mullins, Ireland	P. Townend	6/1
2	2½	THE BIG WESTERNER (IRE)	6	11-0		Henry de Bromhead, Ireland	D. J. O'Keeffe	9/2f
3	4½	DERRYHASSEN PADDY (IRE)	6	11-7	(t)	Lucinda Russell	Derek Fox	10/1
4	hd	YELLOW CAR (IRE)	7	11-7		David Killahena & Graeme McPherson	Nick Slatter	33/1
5	¾	WENDIGO (FR)	6	11-7		Jamie Snowden	Gavin Sheehan	16/1
6	11	JIG'S FORGE (IRE)	6	11-7		Ben Pauling	Ben Jones	125/1
7	5½	MA SHANTOU (IRE)	6	11-7		Emma Lavelle	Harry Cobden	25/1
8	5½	SOUNDS VICTORIOUS (IRE)	6	11-7		W. P. Mullins, Ireland	Mr P. W. Mullins	20/1
9	½	JET BLUE (FR)	6	11-7		David Cottin, France	James Reveley	5/1
10	¾	WINGMEN (IRE)	7	11-7	(h)	Gordon Elliott, Ireland	J. W. Kennedy	6/1
11	40	PORT JOULAIN (FR)	6	11-7		W. P. Mullins, Ireland	B. Hayes	50/1
12	3½	BALLYBOW (IRE)	6	11-7		Gordon Elliott, Ireland	Danny Gilligan	22/1
13	¾	INN AT THE PARK (IRE)	7	11-7		W. P. Mullins, Ireland	D. E. Mullins	66/1
14	25	ARGENTO BOY (IRE)	6	11-7		W. P. Mullins, Ireland	Rachael Blackmore	14/1
pu		FIRST CONFESSION (IRE)	6	11-7		Joe Tizzard	Brendan Powell	50/1
pu		FISHERY LANE (FR)	6	11-7		W. P. Mullins, Ireland	S. F. O'Keeffe	50/1
pu		FLICKER OF HOPE (FR)	6	11-7		Mark Fahey, Ireland	Keith Donoghue	25/1
pu		INTENSE APPROACH	6	11-7		John McConnell, Ireland	Sean Bowen	14/1
pu		JAX JUNIOR	6	11-7		Lucy Wadham	Tom Cannon	22/1
pu		NATIVEHILL (IRE)	7	11-7	(t)	Nicky Henderson	Nico de Boinville	66/1

20 ran Race Time 5m 57.60 Closing Sectional (3.80f): 54.7s (103.6%) Winning Owner: Mr Simon Munir/Mr Isaac Souede

The third of the Grade 1 novice hurdles at the meeting, a race in which the winner's performance tends to be a notch below that of the winners of the Supreme and Baring Bingham, and that was no different on this occasion, the with first 5 a little too closely bunched at the finish to take a high view of the principals; all 20—a maximum field—had won at least once over hurdles, though only 4 of them had won at graded level, and the race looked the most open of the 3 Grade 1 novices, the runner-up sent off 9/2 favourite and narrowly failing to become the first market leader to land the Spa since At Fisher's Cross in 2013, a race which provides a very different test to that most runners in it will have faced having a history of throwing up surprise results; the race was run at a sound pace and, whilst plenty still had a chance 2 out, things got rather messy on the inside soon after as a result, the winner instead coming wide in a repeat of Kargese in the race before, while the strong emphasis on stamina proved too much for plenty from then on, with nearly a third of the field pulled up in the closing stages; it was an encouraging race for British stables. **Jasmin de Vaux** hadn't come up to expectations on his first 2 starts in graded company (tried in cheekpieces time before), but he was strong in the betting on his first visit to Cheltenham since his Champion Bumper win and proved very well suited by this much stiffer test, given a good ride, brought wide and away from the others into the straight, that surely an advantage the way the race unfolded, though he was strong at the finish as well after being challenged at the last; held up, travelled well, not fluent 3 out, rapid headway approaching 2 out, led approaching last, shaken up run-in, kept on well, drew clear final 100 yds; he isn't the most imposing of these and his future may be over hurdles, with plenty of room in the staying division for a younger contender to come through. **The Big Westerner** ran a fine race in defeat making her first start in 11 weeks and only her third in all and might have done even better had she made her move on the outside with the winner, rather than tight around the inside where she met trouble; waited with, travelled well, tracked pace 3 out, hampered approaching 2 out, effort straight, challenged approaching last, edged left, kept on well run-in; she has more about her physically than the winner but is open to further improvement over hurdles before having her eye turned to chasing. **Derryhassen Paddy** has made a fine start over hurdles and progressed again up in grade, his exertions just telling late on, having quite a hard race, which would seem to rule out a tilt at the Sefton in just over 3 weeks; helped force pace, led third and fourth, not fluent eighth, pushed along after, led again 2 out, headed early in straight, one paced, just held third; he's a smashing chasing prospect for next season. **Yellow Car** showed improved form, a shade better than the result after meeting trouble and if anything needing even more of an emphasis on stamina, therefore likely to benefit from a switch to fences, even if he doesn't have so obvious a physique for it as many of these; waited with, effort after 3 out, ridden when hampered after 2 out, outpaced early in straight, kept on well run-in. **Wendigo** ran a fine race under a change of tactics, fully effective at 3m and sure to have done even better without suffering the worst of the trouble on the inside from 2 out; held up, travelled well, headway after 3 out, short of room 2 out, stumbled (almost unseated) and lost place, stayed on again last; he was one of the picks of the paddock in terms of physique and, with his earlier second to The New Lion franked earlier in the week to boot, is a fine chasing prospect for next season. **Jig's Forge** lacked the experience of quite a few of the others and ran about as well as could have been expected upped in grade, impressing with the way he got into contention before his effort flattened out; patiently ridden, good progress after 3 out, every chance 2 out, shaken up after, weakened last; he's made a bright start to his career, highly tried. **Ma Shantou** looked as well as any beforehand and ran respectably up in grade, though he didn't finish the race nearly so well as might have been expected, upsides the winner (away from the trouble) and still going well enough 2 out but not picking up at all in the straight; tracked pace, travelled well, shaken up entering straight, soon done with. **Sounds Victorius** hadn't been that far behind the winner here at Leopardstown, but he was on his toes beforehand and failed to repeat that form, never mind find the improvement needed, perhaps finding the experience too much; in touch, ridden after 3 out, lost place soon after; he should be suited by 3m. **Jet Blue** wasn't in the same form after 3 months off, his cause not helped by being tight on the inside as the field bunched 2 out; held up, brief headway 2 out, short of room soon after, weakening when mistake last,

TIMEFORM'S VIEW

eased. **Wingmen** held solid form claims, having been placed in Grade 1 novices the last twice (ahead of the winner last time), but he ran below form, doing plenty in front and not getting home over the longer trip; pressed leader, went on after fourth, headed when mistake 2 out, shaken up after, weakened approaching last, eased; he's every inch a chaser on looks and should make a smart novice over fences next season provided his quirks hold. **Port Joulain** wasn't sure to stay this much longer trip (on his toes beforehand, too), but he had plenty to find in this company and wasn't up to the task above all; in touch, not fluent fifth, eighth, left behind after 3 out. **Ballybow** ran no sort of race ridden much more patiently than previously over hurdles, perhaps needing softer ground as well to be seen to best advantage; held up, pushed along sixth, labouring after 3 out. **Inn At The Park** has plenty about him physically, but this was a big step up in class and he didn't make much of a fist of it, in trouble a long way from home; soon steadied, mistake fifth, pushed along after, tailed off after 3 out. **Argento Boy** a half-brother to the Champion Bumper winner Briar Hill (who was sent off favourite for this race), has yet to show his sibling's ability and was well held taking a significant step up in class; settled in touch after third, shaken up after 3 out, well behind soon after. **First Confession** has plenty about him physically and has a pedigree that suggests 3m will be right up his street, but he was overfaced in Grade 1 company for the second time; prominent, shaken up 3 out, lost place soon after, tailed off when pulled up before last; he's done well in the right grade as a hurdler and has the makings of a better chaser next season. **Fishery Lane** fifth behind the winner in the Champion Bumper last season, had just 2 runs in maidens to his name over hurdles and wasn't up to the task, though he was sweating badly beforehand and that might well have contributed to his dull performance; mid-division, shaken up after 3 out, weakened after 2 out, pulled up before last. **Flicker of Hope** was unable to reproduce his handicap form back in novice company, never in the hunt; in rear, labouring 3 out, pulled up before last; he has the physique to make a chaser. **Intense Approach** had won 4 times over hurdles, but he had less potential to improve than a lot of these and essentially wasn't up to the task, having looked outclassed in this field on looks beforehand; prominent, hung left, ridden 3 out, weakened soon after, pulled up before last. **Jax Junior** sweating a touch and geed up beforehand, didn't get home stepped up in trip; led first, remained prominent, shaken up before 2 out, mistake there, weakened home turn, pulled up before last. **Nativehill** running for the sponsors, has loads of stamina in his family and will prove effective at 3m another day, but this was just all too much at this early stage of his career after less than 2 weeks off and he was never really going; raced off the pace, labouring early final circuit, tailed off after 3 out, pulled up; he is every inch a chaser and will be a different proposition next winter.

Boodles Cheltenham Gold Cup Chase (Grade 1) (1)

Pos	Btn	Horse	Age	Wgt	Eq	Trainer	Jockey	SP
1		INOTHEWAYURTHINKIN (IRE)	7	11-10	(t)	Gavin Patrick Cromwell, Ireland	M. P. Walsh	15/2
2	6	GALOPIN DES CHAMPS (FR)	9	11-10		W. P. Mullins, Ireland	P. Townend	8/13f
3	12	GENTLEMANSGAME	9	11-10		M. F. Morris, Ireland	D. J. O'Keeffe	40/1
4	1¼	MONTY'S STAR (IRE)	8	11-10		Henry de Bromhead, Ireland	Rachael Blackmore	8/1
5	20	THE REAL WHACKER (IRE)	9	11-10	(t)	Patrick Neville	Brian Hughes	28/1
6	2¼	ROYALE PAGAILLE (FR)	11	11-10		Venetia Williams	Charlie Deutsch	80/1
7	1¼	BANBRIDGE (IRE)	9	11-10	(s)	Joseph Patrick O'Brien, Ireland	J. J. Slevin	13/2

TIMEFORM'S VIEW

| F | AHOY SENOR (IRE) | 10 | 11-10 | Lucinda Russell | Derek Fox | 28/1 |
| F | CORBETTS CROSS (IRE) | 8 | 11-10 | Emmet Mullins, Ireland | J. W. Kennedy | 14/1 |

9 ran Race Time 6m 41.0s Closing Sectional (3.84f): 54.6s (107.2%) Winning Owner: Mr John P. McManus

A Cheltenham Gold Cup that revolved around Galopin des Champs and his bid to become the first 3-time winner since Best Mate at the start of the century, Kauto Star and Al Boum Photo both having failed in their attempts to win for a third time in the interim, and just 9 went to post, the joint-smallest field in the 2000s, though there weren't many obvious contenders missing—L'Homme Presse might have given British stables at least a squeak but the home team mustered just a trio of outsiders in event, even though they included 2 of just 4 that had won a race this season, the Betfair Chase winner Royale Pagaille and Charlie Hall victor The Real Whacker; the main opposition to the favourite looked to be the King George winner Banbridge, but he disappointed and it was left to the youngest runner in the field to progress a chunk to land the spoils, Inothewayurthinkin continuing the run of 7—and 8-y-os in this race, Don Cossack in 2016 the last older than that to win, the lightly-raced winner's performance well up to standard for the race even if probably just behind the beaten favourite's peak. **Inothewayurthinkin** the youngest runner in the line-up, had shaped very well with seemingly the Grand National in mind when behind Galopin des Champs at Leopardstown the last twice but proved to have the improvement in him to land the blue riband of chasing itself, successful in the Fulke Walwyn Kim Muir here last season and well served by the return to the track and the longer distance, running to a level not far behind the best of the favourite's form; held up, mistake first, not fluent at times after, smooth headway after 3 out, led approaching last, quickened clear; he was made a short-priced favourite for the Grand National afterwards, thrown-in on this improved form and looking to have the obvious profile for the modern-day National—he holds outstanding claims to become just the second horse to win the Gold Cup and Grand National in the same season, Golden Miller in 1934 having been the only previous horse to achieve that. **Galopin des Champs** looked to hold strong claims on form but came up short in his bid for a third Gold Cup, not seeming quite himself and running a bit below his best, not going with his customary zest away from the mud (more patiently ridden than when winning the last twice) and not jumping with the flair that he sometimes can; in touch, not fluent seventh, hampered fifteenth, good progress eighteenth, led after 3 out, shaken up next, headed approaching last, one paced run-in; he may well prove vulnerable if sent to Punchestown and another bid in this race next season will surely be the main aim, though he'll be 10 then and no horse of that age has won since Cool Dawn in 1998. **Gentlemansgame** pulled up in last season's Gold Cup and below form in the Cotswold last time, ran a much better race with cheekpieces left off, essentially not good enough rather than beaten for stamina; prominent, left disputing lead fifteenth, mistake seventeenth, headed after 3 out, left behind 2 out; he holds a Grand National entry, though he would be at level weights with the winner should they both take their chance. **Monty's Star** runner-up to Fact To File in the Broadway last season, ran another sound race and might have done a shade better but for one serious error and being hampered by the faller; waited with, bad mistake ninth, hampered fifteenth, tracked pace eighteenth, ridden 3 out, left behind straight. **The Real Whacker** had won the Broadway as a novice, but he'd been pulled up in last season's Gold Cup and was well held this time around back from 11 weeks off; blundered first, went prominent after second, left disputing lead fifteenth, blundered seventeenth, shaken up 4 out, lost place before next, hung left straight. **Royale Pagaille** running in the Gold Cup for the fourth time (best placing when fifth in 2022), didn't have ground soft enough to give him any chance and he was always out the back; dropped out, not always fluent, mistake eleventh, labouring after, lost touch back straight; he's in the Grand National but makes little appeal for that. **Banbridge** not seen since his victory in the King George, was the disappointment of the race and was beaten a long way from home, well before the longer trip came into play; settled in touch from fourth, not fluent seventh, ridden when mistake 4 out, left behind next; he bounced back from a poor run in the Ryanair last season (when the testing ground was an excuse) to win at Punchestown. **Ahoy Senor** was backed at long odds, having had a breathing operation since his last run, but he had been caught out by a ditch when falling in the 2023 running and was again, departing 2 fences earlier; led, not always fluent, jumped right, fell fifteenth. **Corbetts Cross** winner of the last running of the National Hunt Chase as a graded race, met a sad end whilst running respectably under conditions that didn't test his stamina to the full; held up, hampered fifteenth, headway and every chance 3 out, not quicken straight, fell fatally 2 out.

2024/25 STATISTICS (Britain)

HORSES TO FOLLOW

	TRAINERS (1,2,3 earnings)	Horses	Indiv'l Wnrs	Races Won	Runs	% Strike Rate	Stakes £
1	W. P. Mullins, Ireland	139	33	38	204	18.6	3,405,628
2	Dan Skelton	255	118	179	996	18.0	3,083,787
3	Paul Nicholls	156	68	99	550	18.0	2,440,423
4	Nicky Henderson	127	48	75	396	18.9	2,205,462
5	Olly Murphy	152	85	141	570	24.7	1,633,718
6	Nigel Twiston-Davies	115	50	72	459	15.7	1,249,222
7	Venetia Williams	75	28	40	267	15.0	1,205,536
8	Jonjo & A.J. O'Neill	135	50	72	565	12.7	1,105,274
9	Fergal O'Brien	170	63	85	606	14.0	1,103,515
10	Joe Tizzard	84	44	68	374	18.2	1,029,463

	JOCKEYS (by winners)	1st	2nd	3rd	Unpl	Total Rides	% Strike Rate
1	Sean Bowen	180	135	108	479	902	20.0
2	Harry Skelton	142	113	85	333	673	21.1
3	Harry Cobden	116	81	71	281	549	21.1
4	Sam Twiston-Davies	109	102	95	353	659	16.5
5	Gavin Sheehan	106	81	66	300	553	19.2
6	James Bowen	85	83	64	240	472	18.0
7	Brian Hughes	80	102	105	419	706	11.3
8	Jonathan Burke	78	71	72	283	504	15.5
9	Ben Jones	77	81	58	253	469	16.4
10	Danny McMenamin	70	71	58	267	466	15.0

	SIRES OF WINNERS (1,2,3 earnings)	Races Won	Runs	% Strike Rate	Stakes £
1	Walk In The Park (by Montjeu)	93	700	13.3	2,784,675
2	Getaway (by Monsun)	124	909	13.6	1,409,316
3	Mahler (by Galileo)	85	628	13.5	1,060,470
4	Westerner (by Danehill)	64	467	13.7	987,830
5	Kayf Tara (by Sadler's Wells)	54	468	11.5	942,182
6	Martaline (by Linamix)	41	243	16.9	923,235
7	Malinas (by Lomitas)	61	406	15.0	881,122
8	Golden Horn (by Cape Cross)	32	161	19.9	879,838
9	Fame And Glory (by Montjeu)	58	415	14.0	864,894
10	Doyen (by Sadler's Wells)	61	384	15.9	863,722

	LEADING HORSES (1,2,3 earnings)	Races Won	Runs	Stakes £
1	Jonbon 9 b.g Walk In The Park - Star Face	4	6	563,845
2	Nick Rockett 8 b.g Walk In The Park - Eireann Rose	1	1	500,000
3	Inothewayurthinkin 7 b.g Walk In The Park - Sway	1	1	366,198
4	Golden Ace 6 b.f Golden Horn - Deuce Again	2	4	312,798
5	Lossiemouth 6 gr.f Great Pretender - Mariner's Light	2	3	244,643
6	Marine Nationale 8 b.g French Navy - Power Of Future	1	1	234,400
7	Fact To File 8 b.g Poliglote - Mitemps	1	1	212,287
8	I Am Maximus 9 b.g Authorized - Polysheba	0	1	200,000
9	Gaelic Warrior 7 b.g Maxios - Game Of Legs	2	2	189,235
10	Bob Olinger 10 b.g Sholokhov - Zenaide	1	1	182,878

REFERENCE & INDEX

SECTION 5

THE TIMEFORM TOP 100	132
INDEX	134

THE TIMEFORM TOP 100

Hurdlers

167	State Man
166	Constitution Hill
162	Ballyburn
162	Impaire Et Passe
161p	The New Lion
161	Irish Point
160p	Final Demand
160	Bob Olinger
159	Kopek des Bordes
159	Teahupoo
158P	Sir Gino
158	Lossiemouth
158	Sharjah
157	Brighterdaysahead
157?	Il Est Francais
156	William Munny
155	Absurde
155	Hiddenvalley Lake
155	The Yellow Clay
154	Gaelic Warrior
153p	Majborough
153	Flooring Porter
153	Salvator Mundi
153	Strong Leader
152	Asterion Forlonge
152	Ballyadam
152	Daddy Long Legs
152	El Fabiolo
152	Home By The Lee
152	Jimmy du Seuil
152	Minella Cocooner
152	Saint Roi
152	Slade Steel
151p	Anzadam
151	Blueking d'Oroux
151	Gold Tweet
151	Maxxum
151	Ndaawi
151	Rubaud
151x	Zanahiyr
150p	Kitzbuhel
150p	Lulamba
150	Crambo
150	Gentlemansgame
150	Inthepocket
150	Saint Sam
149p	Mister Policeman
149	Beauport
149	Burdett Road
149	Champ Kiely
149	Farouk d'Alene
149	Fastorslow
149	Golden Ace
149	Il Etait Temps
149	Jade de Grugy
149	Jesse Evans
149	Lucky Place
149	Nemean Lion
149	Nurburgring
149	Poniros
149	Quel Destin
149	Romeo Coolio
149	The Wallpark
149	Winter Fog
149	Wodhooh
149?	Mystical Power
148+	East India Dock
148	Dancing City
148	Fil Dor
148	Firefox
148	Good Land
148	Hewick
148	Monkfish
148	Monmiral
148	My Mate Mozzie
148	Quilixios
148	Rocky's Diamond
148	Salver
148	Tommy's Oscar
147p	Caldwell Potter
147	Ashdale Bob
147	Buddy One
147	Dysart Dynamo
147	Galvin
147	Gaucher
147	Irancy
147	Jeriko du Reponet
147	Kargese
147	Luccia
147	Stellar Story
147	Storm Heart
147	The Jukebox Man
147	Thedevilscoachman
146+	Pied Piper
146	Better Days Ahead
146	Happy Jacky
146	Impose Toi
146	Journey With Me
146	Sire du Berlais
146	Telmesomethinggirl

Chasers

175	Galopin des Champs
174+	Inothewayurthinkin
173	Fact To File
172	Gerri Colombe
172	Il Etait Temps
171	Jonbon
169	Gaelic Warrior
168	Fastorslow
168	I Am Maximus
167	Marine Nationale
166	Grangeclare West
166	Nick Rockett
166	Spillane's Tower
166x	El Fabiolo
165	Banbridge
164	Corach Rambler
164	Grey Dawning
164	Quilixios
164?	Noble Yeats
163p	Sir Gino
163	Found A Fifty
163	Heart Wood
163	Il Est Francais
163	Pic d'Orhy
163	Protektorat
163	Solness
162p	Majborough
162	Energumene
162	L'Homme Presse
162?	Royale Pagaille
161	Corbetts Cross
161	Embassy Gardens
161	Envoi Allen
161	Hewick
161	Monty's Star
161	Stage Star
160	Djelo
160	Gentlemansgame
160	Sounds Russian
160?	Bob Olinger
159	Al Dancer
159	Appreciate It
159	Easy Game
159	Ferny Hollow
159	Impaire Et Passe
159	Matata
159	Saint Sam
158	Ballyburn
158	Captain Guinness
158	Champ Kiely
158	Chianti Classico
158	Edwardstone
158	Perceval Legallois
158	Stumptown
158?	Monkfish
157+	Flooring Porter
157	Boothill
157	Gentleman de Mee
157	James du Berlais
157	Jungle Boogie
157	Thunder Rock
157x	Saint Roi
156p	Iroko
156+	Mister Policeman
156	Beauport
156	Classic Getaway
156	Delta Work
156	Dinoblue
156	Jpr One
155p	Gidleigh Park
155p	Kalif du Berlais
155	Jango Baie
155	Lecky Watson
155	Master Chewy
155	Sa Fureur
155	The Real Whacker
155x	Beacon Edge
154+	Sir Gerhard
154	Ga Law

THE TIMEFORM TOP 100 | 133

154	Handstands
154	Juntos Ganamos
154	L'Eau du Sud
154	Minella Cocooner
154	Western Fold
154?	Nassalam
153	Blood Destiny
153	Caldwell Potter
153	Croke Park
153	Galvin
153	Hercule du Seuil
153	Inthepocket
153	Springwell Bay
153	Stolen Silver
152p	Haiti Couleurs
152p	The Jukebox Man
152+	Jingko Blue
152	Better Days Ahead
152	Boombawn
152	Bravemansgame
152	Dancing On My Own
152	Ile Atlantique
152	Pinkerton
152	Quai de Bourbon
152	Sam Brown
152	Stellar Story
152x	Foxy Jacks
152?	Dysart Dynamo
152?	Threeunderthrufive

Juvenile Hurdlers

150p	Lulamba
149	Poniros
148+	East India Dock
145	Nietzsche Has
143	Hello Neighbour
139	Give It To Me Oj
138	Lady Vega Allen
137p	Live Conti
137	Place de La Nation
136	Puturhandstogether
134	Blue Lemons
134	Murcia
134	Willy de Houelle
132	Galileo Dame
132	Stencil
132	Wendrock
130	Bacchanalian

130	Last Kingdom
130	Naturally Nimble
130	Sony Bill
129p	Too Bossy For Us
129	Mambonumberfive
126	Gibbs Island
126	Total Look
125	Sir Galahad
125	St Pancras
124	Larzac
124	Mondo Man
124	Robbies Rock
123	Hot Fuss
123	Teriferma

Novice Hurdlers

161p	The New Lion
160p	Final Demand
159	Kopek des Bordes
156	William Munny
155	The Yellow Clay
153	Salvator Mundi
149	Romeo Coolio
147	Gaucher
147	Irancy
143p	Jasmin de Vaux
143	Ethical Diamond
143	Karniquet
142p	Kawaboomga
142p	Lovely Hurling
142	Karbau
142	Sunchart
141p	Honesty Policy
141	Al Gasparo
141	Tripoli Flyer
140	Forty Coats
140	Potters Charm
138	Air of Entitlement
138	Cashedale Lad
138	Chart Topper
138	Julius des Pictons
137p	Fingle Bridge
137p	Sixandahalf
137	Derryhassen Paddy
137	Shuffle The Deck
137?	Timmy Tuesday

Novice Chasers

163p	Sir Gino
162p	Majborough
159	Impaire Et Passe
158	Ballyburn
158	Champ Kiely
155p	Gidleigh Park
155p	Kalif du Berlais
155	Jango Baie
155	Lecky Watson
154	Handstands
154	L'Eau du Sud
154	Western Fold
153	Caldwell Potter
153	Croke Park
153	Inthepocket
153	Springwell Bay
152p	Haiti Couleurs
152p	The Jukebox Man
152+	Jingko Blue
152	Better Days Ahead
152	Boombawn
152	Ile Atlantique
152	Quai de Bourbon
152	Stellar Story
151	Blizzard of Oz
151	Firefox
150p	Jagwar
150+	High Class Hero
150+	Jordans
150	Jesse Evans

National Hunt Flat Horses

120	Windbeneathmywings
119	Heads Up
117	Colcannon
117	Shuttle Diplomacy
116	Sortudo
115	Bambino Fever
115	Green Splendour
114	El Cairos
113	Baron Noir
113	Copacabana
112p	Doctor du Mesnil
112	Caballero Cliff
112	Idaho Sun

111	Kalypso'chance
111	Ksar Fatal
111	Switch From Diesel
110	Burrows Drive
110	He Can't Dance
109p	Gameofinches
109p	Mydaddypaddy
109	Koktail Brut
109	No Drama This End
108	Cantico
108	Ellen Kelly
107	Aqua Force
107	Carrigmoornaspruce
107	I Started A Joke
107	Sober Glory
107	Soldier In Milan
106p	Starzand
106	Dalston Lad
106	Fortune de Mer

Index

A

Ace of Spades	4
Ahoy Senor	129
Air of Entitlement	117
Allegorie de Vassy	125
Altobelli	80
A Moments Madness	92
Aqua Force	117
Arcadian Emperor	76
Argento Boy	127
Aurora Vega	118

B

Backtonormal	56
Ballybow	127
Ballyburn	113
Bambino Fever	116
Banbridge	97, 129
Battle Born Lad	5
Be Aware	6
Better Days Ahead	113
Bill Joyce	84
Blueking d'Oroux	84
Blue Lemons	124
Bluey	119
Bob Olinger	100, 120
Born In The West	7
Brendas Asking	118
Brides Hill	124
Brighterdaysahead	98, 108
Buddy One	121
Burdett Road	108
Burning It Up	8

C

Caballero Cliff	116
Caesar Rock	111
Califet En Vol	8
Captain Cody	111
Captain Guinness	114
Celtic Dino	10
Charlus	123
Chasingouttheblues	11
Conman Hill	12
Constitution Hill	98, 109
Copacabana	116
Corbetts Cross	129
Crambo	121

D

Dalston Lad	117
Dancing City	114
Dedicated Hero	13
Derryhassen Paddy	14, 126
Dinoblue	124
Diva Luna	15, 118
Djelo	120
Doctor du Mesnil	56
Duffle Coat	111
Dysart Enos	107

E

East India Dock	123
East India Express	81
El Cairos	116
Energumene	115
Envoi Allen	119
Ethical Diamond	57

F

Fact To File	102, 119
Fastorslow	102
Feet of A Dancer	59
Filibustering	80
Final Demand	59, 112
First Confession	127
Fishery Lane	127
Flicker of Hope	127
Fontaine Collonges	125
Fortune de Mer	117
Forty Coats	112
Found A Fifty	115
Franciscan Rock	121
Funiculi Funicula	105

G

Gaelic Warrior	98
Gala Marceau	108
Ga Law	121
Galileo Dame	118
Galopin des Champs	102, 128
Gameofinches	60, 116
Gentlemansgame	128
George's Lad	16
Gericault Roque	110
Gibbs Island	124
Gidleigh Park	80
Gold Cast	92
Golden Ace	108
Gorgeous Tom	113
Gowel Road	121
Grangeclare West	102
Green Hint	77
Grey Dawning	85

H

Haiti Couleurs	17, 109
Hang In There	120
Hasthing	110
Heads Up	116
Heart Wood	119
He Can't Dance	116
Heldam	77
Hello Neighbour	123
Herakles Westwood	110
Hollygrove Cha Cha	119
Home By The Lee	121

I

I Am Maximus	102
Idaho Sun	18, 80, 116
Il Est Francais	97, 120
Il Etait Temps	61
Imperial Saint	82
In d'Or	110
Inn At The Park	127
Inothewayurthinkin	101, 102, 128
Intense Approach	127
Irancy	105
Iroko	102
I Started A Joke	116

J

Jade de Grugy	107
Jagwar	19
Jane Eire	118
Jango Baie	20, 106
Jasmin de Vaux	100, 101, 126
Jax Junior	127
Jesuila des Mottes	22
Je T'ai Porte	125
Jetara	107
Jet Blue	126
Jig's Forge	126
Jingko Blue	81
Job	22
Jonbon	99, 114
Joyeuse	107
Jubilee Alpha	83, 118
Juby Ball	23
July Flower	107
Jungle Boogie	120
Jupiter Allen	110
Jupiter des Bordes	24
Jurancon	85
Just A Rose	119

K

Kabral du Mathan	25
Kaid d'Authie	112
Kala Conti	107
Kalif du Berlais	83, 99, 100
Kalypso'chance	116
Kappa Jy Pyke	112
Karamoja	118
Karbau	105
Karl des Tourelles	63
Karniquet	63, 105
Karoline Banbou	118
Kawaboomga	64
Kel Histoire	112
Kepler's Law	26
Kibris	78
Kimi de Mai	118
King of Kingsfield	108
Kingston Pride	92
Kingston Queen	27
Kiss Will	112
Kitty Foyle	118
Klarc Kent	110
Kopeck de Mee	65
Kopek des Bordes	104
Krak	78
Kyntara	111

L

Lady Vega Allen	123
Lagertha	118
Lancelot Allen	117
Lanesborough	84
Larzac	124
Last Rodeo	28
Laughing John	81
L'Eau du Sud	106
Lecky Watson	98, 113
Le Frimeur	79
Le Tiep's Sacre	29
Libberty Hunter	115
Limerick Lace	124
Lombron	66
Lossiemouth	107
Lovely Hurling	67
Love Sign D'Aunou	76
Lucky Place	81, 121
Lulamba	29, 122
Lumiere du Large	123

M

Macao	93
Magic McColgan	118
Majborough	99, 106
Marine Nationale	99, 114
Ma Shantou	126
Master Chewy	120
Maughreen	119
Mayhem Mya	124
Metkayina	118
Miami Magic	31
Mighty Park	76
Mister Meggit	84
Monbeg Genius	84
Mondo Man	123
Monty's Star	128
Mossy Fen Coolio	84
Mossy Fen Road	80
Mydaddypaddy	32, 86
Myretown	33
Mystical Goddess	118

INDEX

Mystical Power	122

N

Narciso Has	94
Nativehill	94, 127
Native Speaker	68
Nemean Lion	122
Nick Rockett	102
No Drama This End	34, 116
Norn Iron	80
No Time To Wait	110
Now Is The Hour	111

O

Only By Night	106
Opec	124
Our Boy Stan	35

P

Pappano	124
Phantomofthepoints	84
Pic Roc	84
Place de La Nation	69, 123
Poetisa	95
Poniros	122
Port Joulain	127
Potters Charm	112
Pourquoi Pas Papa	95
Protektorat	120
Push The Button	95

Q

Quai de Bourbon	114
Quantum Quest	79
Queenie St Clair	118
Queens Gamble	108
Quilixios	115

R

Raffles Dolce Vita	79
Realco	37
Resplendent Grey	110
Rock My Way	110
Rocky's Diamond	121
Romeo Coolio	104
Royale Margaux	125
Royale Pagaille	129
Rubber Ball	38

S

Sainte Lucie	123
Salvator Mundi	105
Senator	86
Shecouldbeanything	124
Shuttle Diplomacy	116
Sixandahalf	118
Sixmilebridge	112
Skuna Bay	39
Sky Lord	105
Sober Glory	82
Soldier In Milan	70
Soldier's Leap	40
Solness	114
Some Bro	41
Sortudo	116
Sounds Victorious	126
Spread Boss Ted	71
Starzand	41, 82
State Man	98, 109
Stellar Story	72, 113
Strong Run	42
Stuzzikini	111
Supersundae	112

T

Take No Chances	107
Teahupoo	100, 121
Terrorise	43
The Big Westerner	126
Thecompanysergeant	73
The Jukebox Man	98
The New Lion	44, 85, 99, 111
The Real Whacker	128
The Wallpark	121
The Yellow Clay	112
Tiptoptim	86
Tom Doniphon	45
Too Bossy For Us	123
Touch Me Not	106
Tour Ovalie	118
Transmission	110
Tutti Quanti	46, 105

V

Vanderpoel	47, 84
Venusienne	118
Vitorio Piel	74

W

Walk Tall	49
Wellington Arch	50
Wendigo	50, 86, 126
Will Do	110
William Munny	104
Willy de Houelle	123
Wilstar	51
Windbeneathmywings	85
Wingmen	127
Winter Fog	108
Wolf Moon	52
Workahead	105

Y

Yellow Car	126
Young Getaway	54

Z

Zekret	96

Index To Photographers

Caption	Photographer	Page
Califet En Vol did too much too soon in the Sefton but remains a fine prospect for chasing	PA Images	9
Derryhassen Paddy (left) showed a fine attitude when battling to win at Windsor	PA Images	14
Haiti Couleurs forged clear in the Irish Grand National to cap an outstanding campaign	PA Images	18
Jango Baie (right) powered home to snatch victory from the jaws of defeat in the Arkle	PA Images	21
Kabral du Mathan (near side) was only narrowly denied in a thrilling finish to the Scottish Champion Hurdle	PA Images	25
Lulamba (left) was only narrowly denied at Cheltenham but gained revenge at Punchestown	PA Images	30
Myretown proved well ahead of his mark in the Ultima Handicap Chase at Cheltenham	PA Images	33
Our Boy Stan built on his debut promise when a game winner at Kempton	PA Images	36
Rubber Ball (left) won at Newbury during a promising novice hurdle campaign	PA Images	38
Harry Skelton celebrates The New Lion's victory in the Turners Novices' Hurdle	PA Images	45
Vanderpoel strode to an effortless success at Ludlow and is open to improvement	PA Images	48
Wolf Moon (left) has plenty of size about him and should do well over fences	PA Images	53
The form Ethical Diamond showed to win the Sky Bet Ebor suggests he's on a lenient mark over hurdles	PA Images	58
Il Etait Temps proved better than ever when winning the Celebration Chase	PA Images	62
Lombron (left) ran a cracker when runner-up in the Bet365 Gold Cup and is unexposed as a staying chaser	PA Images	67
Stellar Story (left) had to dig deep to make a winning start over fences	PA Images	72
Patrick Mullins celebrates with his father, Willie, after winning the Grand National on Nick Rockett	PA Images	76
Green Hint (green silks) showed promise when chasing home Wonderful Everyday and has joined Willie Mullins	PA Images	77
Daryl Jacob remains a key part of the Munir and Souede operation	PA Images	78
Daryl Jacob pictured winning aboard Intense Raffles for Tom Gibney	PA Images	79
Altobelli (left) has developed a good record at Ascot	PA Images	83
Lucky Place is considered an exciting chasing prospect by connections	PA Images	84
Jubilee Alpha (centre) won three times during a successful novice hurdle campaign	PA Images	85
Windbeneathmywings produced a sparkling performance at Ascot where he proved in a league of his own	PA Images	87
Kingston Pride is still lightly raced and could have more to offer	PA Images	95
Push The Button (grey) was only narrowly beaten at Windsor and should make a chaser for his new yard	PA Images	98
The Jukebox Man impressed when landing the Kauto Star Novices' Chase at Kempton	PA Images	99
Kalif du Berlais signed off for the season with a Grade 1 victory in the Maghull Novices' Chase	PA Images	101
Jasmin de Vaux improved when upped in trip for the Albert Bartlett Novices' Hurdle	PA Images	102
Inothewayurthinkin was a dominant winner of the Cheltenham Gold Cup	PA Images	103

UNMISSABLE CONTENT DELIVERED DAILY

Join today to access exclusive premium articles and expert tips, plus Race Replays, My Stable Tracker, Racecards+ and more.

SPORTING LIFE PLUS
Delivered daily, all completely free.

Scan here